Baccarat®

E E E

CW01651357

TEEL

stockpot with glass lid

ENCAPSULATED BASE CONSTRUCTION
The aluminium core and stainless steel encapsulated base ensures efficient and rapid heat transfer.

STAINLESS STEEL HANDLES
Designed large enough to suit oven gloves and pot holders, perfect for professional style kitchens.

STAINLESS STEEL BODY
Quality stainless steel body with mirror finished, polished exterior surface which is easy to clean and will last a lifetime of use.

LIDS
Lid that fit perfectly, with tempered glass steam vented lid.

COOKTOP SUITABILITY
Suitable for all cooktops including induction, Dishwasher safe.

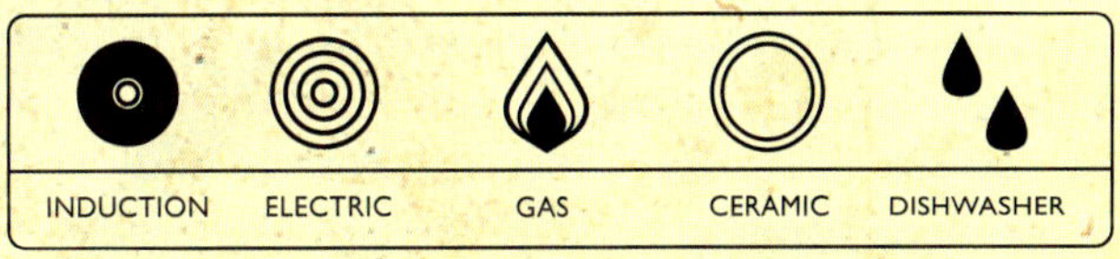

24 x 18cm /8L | 28 x 20cm /12L | 30 x 24cm /16.5L

Published by:
R&R Publications Marketing Pty. Ltd
ABN 78 348 105 138
PO Box 254, Carlton North, Victoria 3054 Australia
Phone (61 3) 9381 2199 Fax (61 3) 9381 2689
E-mail: info@randrpublications.com.au
Website: www.randrpublications.com.au
Australia wide toll free: 1800 063 296

Fresh & Tasty Supa soups (Reproduced as BACCARAT Soup Kitchen)

Publisher: Richard Carroll
Creative Director: Aisling Gallagher
Cover Designer: Leigh Scholten
Additional design: Leigh Scholten
Typeset by Elain Wei Voon Loh
Production Manager: Anthony Carroll
Food Photography: Steve Baxter, Phillip Wilkins, David Munns, Thomas Odulate, Christine Hanscomb and Frank Wieder
Home Economists: Sara Buenfeld, Emma Patmore, Nancy McDougall, Louise Pickford, Jane Stevenson, Oded Schwartz, Alison Austin and Jane Lawrie
Food Stylists: Helen Payne, Sue Russell, Sam Scott, Antonia Gaunt and Oded Schwartz
Recipe Development: Terry Farris, Jacqueline Bellefontaine, Becky Johnson, Valerie Barrett, Emma Patmore, Geri Richards, Pam Mallender and Jan Fullwood
Proofreader: Paul Hassing

Disclaimer: The nutritional information listed with each recipe does not include the nutrient content of garnishes or any accompaniments not listed in specific quantities in the ingredient list. The nutritional information for each recipe is an estimate only, and may vary depending on the brand of ingredients used, and due to natural biological variations in the composition of natural foods such as meat, fish, fruit and vegetables. The nutritional information was calculated by using the computer program Foodworks dietary analysis software (version 3.01, Xyris Software Pty. Ltd. Queensland Australia), and is based on the Australian food composition tables and food manufacturers' data. Where not specified, ingredients are always analysed as average or medium, not small or large. The analysis shown is for 100g of the recipe specified.

Includes Index
ISBN 1 74022 445 0
EAN 9 781740 224 451

First Edition printed September 2004
Second Edition printed January 2006
This Edition printed February 2010
Computer Typeset in Rosewood, Cambria

Printed in Singapore

Cover: Chicken Vegetable page 56

65

CONTENTS

49

56

INTRODUCTION

WHILE SOUP IS VERY EASY TO MAKE AND DELIGHTFULLY SATISFYING TO EAT, THERE IS NO DOUBT THAT A FEW TRICKS OF THE TRADE AND SOME HANDY HINTS WILL GIVE YOU SUPERIOR RESULTS, EVEN IF YOU HAVE NEVER MADE A POT OF SOUP BEFORE.

COOKWARE

Essentially a good stockpot is all you need equipment wise to create delicious and tasty soups.
The Baccarat stockpot is the perfect ingredient in a super soup. It's thick encapsulated aluminium base and stainless steel body ensure an even heat across the whole pot making a great soup even easier to achieve.

INGREDIENTS

We all want to use the best, freshest ingredients when we prepare foods for our family or friends, and there is no doubt that quality ingredients contribute towards a more delicious and healthy end result. Meat, fish, poultry, spices and herbs should always be in peak condition for the best soups. Vegetables, however, can be a little wilted or past their prime. When you are about to make a soup or stock, clean out your vegetable crisper and see what has been left behind. Of course, common sense should prevail, so don't use any vegetables that smell unpleasant or are mouldy.

STOCKS

The basis of a quality soup is a quality stock, it's as simple as that! In years past, a good soup always began with hours of simmering simple vegetables and, perhaps, some meat bones to create a rich broth.

These days, however, if you prefer to bypass this step, there are several prepared stocks available from your local supermarket. They can be found in liquid form, as a paste or as a powder.

Generally speaking, it is much better to purchase liquid stocks as they have a true flavour and are literally ready to use. Pastes are a good option too because they are concentrated, which allows you to add as much water as necessary to dilute the flavour according to your tastes. Most stock powders should be avoided if the liquid or paste stocks are available. These powders are often heavily salted and therefore offer a salty rather than 'true to taste' flavour. The ratio of powder to water can be difficult to master and some brands contain artificial flavours and colours.

By far the most rewarding and delicious stock is the one you make yourself. Contrary to popular belief, stocks are not difficult to make and, although they need to simmer for quite some time, their preparation time is minimal.

The recipes on pages 5 and 6 will guide you through the basics of making a good stock – regardless of which type of stock you wish to make, you can follow one of these basic methods. If you have any vegetables in your refrigerator that are looking a little wilted and sad, throw these into the stockpot too as they will add extra flavour and colour.

Oh, and one other thing – remember that stocks freeze extremely well for extended periods of time, so don't be afraid to make a pot of stock when you have large amounts of vegetables, roasted meat bones or turkey frames (from the Christmas bird) on hand. Make the stock and pop it in the freezer for your future risotto or soup.

RICH VEGETABLE STOCK

In addition to the vegetables below, you can add any other vegetables in your refrigerator that are past their prime; greens, root vegetables, corn and capsicums all work well. The stock freezes beautifully for up to 12 months.

Ingredients

2 tbsp olive oil
1 turnip or yellow turnip
5 cloves garlic
3 sticks celery
3 large carrots
10 mushrooms
3 large onions
4 tomatoes
2 leeks, well washed
10 sprigs parsley
2 parsnips
1 tsp peppercorns
8 brussel sprouts
4 bay leaves

Method

1. Wash all the vegetables and slice or chop roughly. Heat the olive oil in a large stockpot and sauté all the vegetables for 20 minutes until they begin to develop a golden colour on the surface.
2. Add the parsley, peppercorns, bay leaves and water to cover (about 16 cups) and bring to the boil. Simmer for 3 hours, skimming the surface to remove any scum that accumulates.
3. Add salt to taste, then simmer for a further few minutes if you would like a more intense flavour. Allow to cool then strain, pressing on the solids. Use within 3 days or freeze for up to 12 months.

CHICKEN, BEEF AND FISH STOCK

Common Ingredients

2 carrots
4 sticks celery
3 onions
8 sprigs parsley
1 leek
1 tsp peppercorns

Chicken Stock

To the above ingredients, add 2 kg of chicken frames or wings and place all the vegetables and chicken in a large stockpot. Add water to generously cover the ingredients (about 16 cups). Bring to the boil then simmer for 2–3 hours, skimming the scum off the surface as it rises to the top. Add salt to taste, then strain through a sieve lined with paper towels or cheesecloth. Place in a large stockpot and chill until the fat solidifies on the surface. Remove the fat and use the stock or freeze.

Beef Stock

Place 2 kg of beef bones in a roasting pan and roast at 220°C for 1 hour. Then place in a large stockpot with the common vegetable ingredients. Cover with cold water (about 16 cups), bring to the boil and simmer for 2–3 hours, skimming the scum off the surface as it rises to the top. Add salt to taste, then strain through a sieve lined with paper towels or cheesecloth. Place in a large stockpot and chill until the fat solidifies on the surface. Remove the fat and use the stock or freeze.

Fish Stock

Using the common vegetable ingredients, follow the recipe for Rich Vegetable Stock (page 5) then, when adding the vegetables to the stockpot, also add 2 kg of flathead heads (or other white ocean fish heads). Cover with cold water (about 12 cups), bring to the boil and simmer for 2 hours, skimming the scum off the surface as it rises to the top. Add salt to taste, then strain through a sieve lined with paper towels or cheesecloth. Place in a large stockpot and chill until the fat solidifies on the surface. Remove the fat and use the stock or freeze.

MEDITERRANEAN MAGIC

THE DISTINCTLY MEDITERRANEAN FLAVOUR OF THESE SOUPS IS IMPOSSIBLE TO RESIST. TEMPT YOUR PALATE WITH AROMAS OF FRESH TOMATOES AND CAPSICUMS, GARLIC AND HERBS. ADD FRESHLY GRATED CHEESE AND WARM BREAD FOR A DELICIOUS EXPERIENCE LIKE NO OTHER. OR TRY THE CHILLED YOGHURT SOUP FOR AN ENTIRELY DIFFERENT, BUT EQUALLY DELICIOUS, MEDITERRANEAN TASTE. LET YOUR SENSES BE YOUR GUIDE.

MINESTRONE PIEMONTE

Preparation 20 mins + soaking **Cooking** 24 hrs 40 mins **Calories** 46 **Fat** 2g

$^1/_2$ cup small white beans
$^1/_2$ cup kidney beans
$^1/_2$ cup chickpeas
4 white onions, chopped
2 cloves garlic, minced
3 tbsps olive oil
$^1/_2$ small cabbage, sliced
2 sticks celery, sliced
2 medium carrots, sliced finely
6 cups good quality beef stock
2 tbsps tomato paste
12 basil leaves, chopped
6 sprigs parsley
3 bay leaves (fresh if possible)
salt and pepper to taste
100g piece Parmesan rind
4 zucchini, sliced
1 cup good red wine

1. The night before, mix the white beans, kidney beans and chickpeas together and soak in cold water overnight. (If you don't have time to soak the beans overnight, cover them with hot water for 2 hours then drain and proceed with the recipe).
2. Sauté the onions and garlic in the olive oil for 5 minutes or until soft. Add the cabbage, celery and carrots and sauté for a further 5 minutes or until the vegetables have softened.
3. Add the beef stock, tomato paste, soaked bean mixture, basil, parsley, bay leaves and salt and pepper to taste and simmer for 2 hours or until thick and fragrant. Add the Parmesan cheese rind, sliced zucchini, red wine and a little extra water if necessary to thin the soup. Cook for a further 30 minutes, remove bay leaves and serve.

Serves 4

Note: A particularly nice touch is to finish each bowl with a spoonful of pesto. The heat of the soup warms the pesto and allows it to permeate throughout the entire bowl of soup.

MIXED BEAN SOUP

Preparation 8 mins **Cooking** 1 hr 20 mins **Calories** 431 **Fat** 2g

85g dried kidney beans
85g dried cannellini beans
2 tbsps olive oil
55g bacon, chopped
1 onion, chopped
1 clove garlic, crushed
3 stalks celery, sliced
2 carrots, chopped
2 potatoes, chopped
6 cups chicken or vegetable stock
400g canned tomatoes, undrained and mashed
1/4 cabbage, finely shredded
55g small pasta shapes or rice
1 tsp dried mixed herbs
freshly ground black pepper
Parmesan cheese, grated

1. Place kidney and cannellini beans in a bowl. Cover with cold water and set aside to soak overnight. Drain.
2. Heat oil in a stockpot over a medium heat, add bacon, onion and garlic and cook, stirring, for 5 minutes or until onion is tender. Add celery, carrots and potatoes and cook for 1 minute longer.
3. Stir in the stock, tomatoes, cabbage, pasta or rice, kidney and cannellini beans, herbs and black pepper to taste and bring to the boil. Boil for 10 minutes, then reduce the heat and simmer, stirring occasionally, for 1 hour or until the beans are tender. Sprinkle with Parmesan cheese and serve.

Serves 4

Note: Extra vegetables of your choice may be added – it is a good way to use up vegetable leftovers.

CHICKEN SOUP

Preparation 15 mins **Cooking** 1 hr **Calories** 105 **Fat** 4g

- 2 rashers bacon, finely chopped
- 1 onion, finely chopped
- 1/2 cup diced celery
- 1/2 cup diced carrot
- 500g chicken thigh pieces
- 750mL water
- salt and pepper
- 2 tbsps parsley, chopped

1. Cook bacon in large stockpot for 2–3 minutes. Add all remaining ingredients, except parsley, bring to boil, simmer gently for 40 minutes.
2. Remove thighs from stockpot. Remove skin and bones, discard. Cut meat into small pieces.
3. Skim fat from surface of the soup. Return chicken meat to stockpot, reheat.
4. Sprinkle with parsley and serve with crusty bread.

Serves 4

ROASTED TOMATO, RED CAPSICUM & BREAD SOUP

Preparation 10 mins **Cooking** 50 mins **Calories** 172 **Fat** 2g

- 1 kg Roma tomatoes, roasted
- 2 red capsicums, roasted and roughly chopped
- 40mL olive oil
- 2 onions, finely chopped
- 3 cloves garlic, crushed
- 2 tsps cumin, ground
- 1 tsp coriander, ground
- 4 cups chicken stock
- 2 slices white bread, crusts removed and torn into pieces
- 1 tbsp balsamic vinegar
- salt and freshly ground pepper, to taste

1. Preheat the oven.
2. Lightly oil a baking dish, place tomatoes in the dish and bake for 20 minutes, (or until the skins have blistered). Set aside to cool, then remove the skins and roughly chop.
3. Heat the oil in a stockpot, add the garlic and the onion, and cook for 5 minutes, or until soft. Add cumin and coriander, and cook for 1 minute, until well combined. Add tomatoes, capsicums and stock to the stockpot, bring to the boil, and simmer (for 30 minutes). Add bread, balsamic vinegar and salt and pepper, and cook for a further 5–10 minutes.
4. Serve with Parmesan cheese, if desired.

Serves 4

Oven temperature 220°C, 440°F, Gas 7

PORCINI MUSHROOM SOUP

Preparation 10 mins **Cooking** 50 mins **Calories** 168 **Fat** 4g

- 1 tbsp dried Porcini
- 1/2 cup boiling water
- 2 tbsps olive oil
- 2 cloves garlic, minced
- 1 leek, cleaned and chopped
- 6 shallots, chopped
- 285g white mushrooms
- 500g forest mushrooms, including porcini, shiitake, oyster and swiss brown
- 2 tbsps flour
- 4 cups good quality chicken, beef or vegetable stock
- 1 cup double cream
- 1/2 bunch flat-leaf parsley, chopped
- 30 basil leaves, sliced
- 1 tbsp fresh oregano
- salt, pepper and nutmeg, to taste

1. Add the dried Porcini to the boiling water and set aside. When the mushrooms have softened, remove them from the mushroom water and set aside. Strain the mushroom liquid through a paper towel or muslin-lined sieve to separate sand and grit, and reserve the liquid.
2. Heat the olive oil and add the garlic, leeks and shallots and cook until golden (about 3 minutes). Add all the fresh mushrooms, thinly sliced, and cook over a very high heat until the mushrooms soften and their liquid evaporates (about 6 minutes). Reserve a few mushroom pieces for a garnish.
3. Sprinkle with the flour and stir well to enable the flour to be absorbed. Add the chicken stock and the Porcini mushrooms together with the soaking liquid and bring to the boil, stirring frequently.
4. Once the soup is boiling, reduce the heat to a simmer and cook for 30 minutes. Add the cream and simmer for a further 5 minutes or until slightly thickened. Add half the chopped parsley, sliced basil and oregano and season to taste with salt and pepper.
5. To serve, ladle into individual bowls, sprinkle with extra parsley, reserved mushrooms, some nutmeg and a small dollop of extra cream if desired.

Serves 6

Note: To make a low-fat version of this delicious soup, substitute evaporated skim milk instead of the cream.

GAZPACHO

Preparation 15 mins **Cooking** none **Calories** 110 **Fat** 4g

- 2 slices of stale bread (optional)
- 2 kg tomatoes, washed and roughly chopped
- 1 cucumber, peeled and chopped
- 1 green capsicum, seeded and chopped
- 1 small onion, peeled and chopped
- 2 cloves garlic, peeled and chopped
- 5 tbsps olive oil
- 1–2 tbsps good wine vinegar, to taste
- 1 tsp cumin seeds or cumin powder
- ice cubes to cool

1. Soak bread (if using) in a little water, and squeeze it out before using. (The bread helps to thicken the soup and give it a nice consistency).
2. Blend all vegetables and garlic in a mixer, and push through a sieve into a bowl. Use the mixer again to beat bread, oil and vinegar together. Add some of the tomatoes, the cumin seeds and salt to taste. Add a little water and mix into the bowl with the soup. Add a few ice cubes and leave to become cold. You can add more water if necessary.

Serves 6–8

Note: Traditionally this soup was made by crushing the ingredients with a mortar and pestle and then adding cold water. Gazpacho should be served in wooden bowls and eaten with a wooden spoon. Make large quantities of Gazpacho as it keeps well – but it won't last long, as you are bound to keep sipping it!

ABALONE CHOWDER

Preparation 20 mins **Cooking** 1 hr **Calories** 115 **Fat** 6g

- 2 rashers bacon (cut into $2^1/_2$cm pieces)
- 1 medium onion, chopped
- 3 tsps freshly crushed garlic
- 2 sticks celery, chopped
- 1 large carrot, chopped
- $^1/_2$ tsp freshly chopped chilli
- 440g can tomato pieces
- 2 tbsps tomato paste
- 2 bay leaves
- 1 heaped tsp thyme leaves
- $^1/_2$ tsp salt
- $^1/_2$ tsp black peppercorns, freshly ground
- 1 cup basic fish stock
- 6 cups water
- 500g abalone steaks, ground or finely chopped
- 2 medium Pontiac potatoes, diced
- 2 tbsps plain flour
- 2 tbsps water
- 2 ice cubes
- $^1/_2$ cup dry sherry

1. Fry bacon in a large frypan (until crisp). Pour off almost all fat, keeping a small amount. Fry onion, garlic, celery, carrot and chilli in the remaining bacon fat.
2. Cook for 3–4 minutes (until vegetables are tender). Transfer to your stockpot. Add the tomatoes, including the juice, tomato paste, bay leaves, thyme and salt and pepper. Stir in the fish stock, water, abalone and potatoes. Bring the mixture to the boil, then reduce heat to simmer. Simmer uncovered for 40–45 minutes.
3. In a jar with a tight-fitting lid, combine the flour, water and ice cubes. Shake the jar vigorously, then pour the flour and water paste into the chowder. Add the sherry. Stir and increase the heat (until the liquid boils). Allow the mixture to boil gently (until the broth thickens slightly).
4. Taste for seasoning, and add more sherry and salt and pepper (if desired).

Serves 10

CHICKPEA, ROASTED TOMATO AND GARLIC SOUP

Preparation 15 mins + soaking **Cooking** 30 mins **Calories** 556 **Fat** trace

500g dried chickpeas
1 kg Roma tomatoes
1 bulb garlic
75mL olive oil
salt
2 tbsps dried oregano
2 leeks, sliced, white part only
4 cups chicken stock
2 tbsps tomato paste
salt and pepper
oregano leaves, fresh

1. Soak chickpeas in cold water overnight. Place chickpeas in a stockpot covered with water and bring to the boil, then simmer for approximately 1 hour until chickpeas are cooked. Drain and set aside.
2. Preheat the oven. Halve the tomatoes and place them in a baking tray. Cut the top off the garlic bulb and place it in the baking tray.
3. Drizzle with olive oil, sprinkle with salt and dried oregano, and roast in the oven for 20–30 minutes.
4. Place the tomatoes and 5 peeled garlic cloves (reserve the rest) in a food processor, and purée for 1 minute.
5. Heat half the oil and sauté the leeks for 3 minutes. Add the stock, and bring to the boil, then reduce heat to simmer.
6. Add the tomato mixture, tomato paste and the chickpeas, season with salt and pepper, and heat through.
7. Sprinkle with fresh oregano leaves just before serving.

Serves 4

Oven temperature 200°C, 400°F, Gas 6

PAPPA AL POMODORO

Preparation 10 mins **Cooking** 1 hr **Calories** 588 **Fat** 5g

- 7 cups good quality vegetable, chicken or beef stock
- 6 tbsps olive oil
- 2 onions, peeled and roughly chopped
- 3 cloves garlic, minced
- 2 red capsicums, finely chopped
- 1 1/3 kg ripe tomatoes, preferably home-grown
- 2 tbsps tomato paste
- 400g stale country bread
- 1/2 bunch fresh basil, roughly torn
- salt and freshly ground pepper, to taste

1. Heat the stock in a stockpot and allow to simmer.
2. Heat the olive oil and add the onion, garlic and capsicums and cook until softened. Add the roughly chopped tomatoes and tomato paste and cook over a medium heat for 10 minutes. Purée this mixture then return it to the stockpot.
3. Remove the crusts from the bread and discard them. Dice the bread into small cubes.
4. To the tomato mixture, add the stock, together with the bread, basil and salt and pepper to taste.
5. Cover and simmer for about 45 minutes, then stir vigorously with a wooden spoon to break up the bread cubes.
6. Serve either hot or at room temperature, with a few extra pieces of basil and some freshly ground black pepper.

Serves 4

Note: For a smoother texture, purée the soup briefly to break up some of the bread cubes, but be careful not to over-process the soup.

MOROCCAN HARIRA

Preparation 12 mins + soaking **Cooking** 1hr 15 mins **Calories** 452 **Fat** 7g

125g chickpeas, washed and picked over and soaked overnight
2 tbsps butter
$1^{1}/_{2}$ tsps cinnamon
1 tsp minced ginger
1 tsp ground turmeric
1 tsp ground paprika
$^{1}/_{2}$ tsp ground black pepper
pinch of saffron threads
500g lamb fillets or shoulder, cut into cubes
1 large onion, finely chopped
$^{1}/_{3}$ cup chopped Italian parsley
$^{1}/_{3}$ cup chopped coriander
400g chopped canned tomatoes
5–6 cups water
125g lentils, washed and picked over
2 tbsps lemon juice
salt to taste
chopped parsley, to garnish

1. In a large stockpot, melt the butter and stir in the cinnamon, ginger, turmeric, paprika, pepper and saffron threads. Cook slowly for 2 minutes to release their wonderful fragrances.
2. Add the cubed lamb, onion, Italian parsley and coriander and cook, stirring, until the lamb is brown and the onions are soft (about 15 minutes). Add the tomatoes and cook a further 5 minutes. Add the water and chickpeas and heat to boiling point. Simmer for 1 hour, partially covered.
3. Add the lentils and cook a further 45 minutes until the lentils are soft. Add lemon juice and salt and cook for a further 5 minutes. Serve with extra lemon slices and parsley if desired.

Serves 4

Note: This traditional Muslim soup is served often during the month-long Ramadan when Muslims fast from sun up to sundown and therefore need a hearty evening meal.

SPANISH PEA SOUP

Preparation 8 mins + standing **Cooking** 3 hrs 20 mins **Calories** 201 **Fat** trace

2 cups dried green split peas
3 cups water
1 tbsp olive oil
1 tbsp Spanish paprika
2 cups chopped onion
1 clove garlic, minced
1 cup chopped green capsicum
3/4 cup thinly sliced carrot
3 medium red potatoes, peeled and cubed
8 cups of chicken or vegetable stock
salt and pepper, to taste
low-fat yoghurt to garnish
2 ears of fresh corn
1/2 bunch chives

1. Pick over the peas and rinse thoroughly. Place them in a large pot, cover with the water and bring to the boil. Simmer for 2 minutes then remove from the heat and cover, and let stand for 1 hour.
2. Meanwhile, heat the oil in a large stockpot and add the Spanish paprika, chopped onion and garlic and saute for 5 minutes until the mixture is fragrant and the onions have softened.
3. Add the green pepper, carrot and chopped potato. Toss the vegetables thoroughly with the onion/paprika mixture until well coated, then continue to cook for 10 minutes, stirring thoroughly during the cooking.
4. Add the stock and salt and pepper to taste then simmer, uncovered, 2–3 hours or until peas are very tender.
5. Cut the kernels off the corn cobs. Reserve 1/2 cup of corn, then add the remainder to the soup and simmer for 2 minutes. Purée the soup until thick and smooth, then serve with a few scattered corn kernels and some chopped chives on top.

Serves 8–10

TRADITIONAL FRENCH ONION SOUP

Preparation 8 mins **Cooking** 1 hr 15 mins **Calories** 207 **Fat** 9g

8 large onions
4 tbsps sherry or port
100g butter or oil
8 rounds of bread
2 cloves garlic, minced
1/2 cup grated Gruyère cheese
1 1/2 tbsps plain flour
1/2 cup grated Parmesan cheese
1 tbsp sugar
salt and pepper, to taste
4 cups good quality beef stock
1/2 cup finely chopped parsley
2–3 cups water
1/2 cup red wine

1. Peel and slice the onions into rounds. Heat the butter (or oil) and sauté the garlic and onions until they are shiny and golden brown (about 15 minutes). Add the flour and stir to allow the flour to absorb the butter residue.
2. Add the sugar, beef stock, water and wine and bring to the boil, then simmer for 45 minutes. Add the sherry and simmer 5 minutes more. Add salt and pepper to taste.
3. Grill the bread until golden. Meanwhile, mix the two cheeses and parsley in a bowl. Place a large tablespoon of cheese mixture on each round of grilled bread and grill until cheese is hot and bubbling.
4. Place one round of bread in each soup bowl and then ladle boiling soup over. The crouton will rise to the top of the bowl. Serve immediately.

Serves 8

SUCCULENT SEAFOOD

SOMEHOW SEAFOOD ALWAYS SEEMS TO BE THE PERFECT INGREDIENT FOR A SOUP. THE SUBTLE, DELICATE FLAVOUR OF FISH COMBINES BEAUTIFULLY WITH THE FRESH HERBS AND SPICES USED IN THESE RECIPES. FROM PRAWNS TO MUSSELS, CALAMARI TO OYSTERS, CRABS TO CLAMS - THESE TEMPTING CHOICES ARE BOTH DELICIOUS AND DECEPTIVELY SIMPLE TO MAKE.

CREAMY LOBSTER CHOWDER

Preparation 5 mins **Cooking** 10–12 mins + reheating **Calories** 316 **Fat** 14g

- $1^1/_2$ cups lobster meat, diced
- 2 tbsps quick cooking rice
- 1 tsp salt
- $^1/_4$ tsp pepper
- $^1/_4$ tsp paprika
- 1 tbsp onion, finely minced
- 2 cups milk
- 2 cups light cream
- 2 tbsps butter

1. Combine rice, salt, pepper, paprika, onion, milk and cream in a stockpot. Cook over medium heat, stirring frequently, for 10–12 minutes, or until the rice softens.
2. Stir in the lobster and the butter. Remove from heat, cool and store in the refrigerator. Just before serving, reheat the chowder over a medium heat, stirring frequently.

Serves 4–6

Note: This soup is best 'aged' for at least 5 hours before serving, so prepare it well ahead of time.

SPICED FISH, TOMATO AND CHICKPEA SOUP

Preparation 15 mins + standing Cooking 35 mins Calories 346 Fat 10g

- 1 tbsp olive oil
- 1 onion, chopped
- 1 tsp ground coriander
- 1 tsp ground cumin
- 1 tsp allspice
- 1 green chilli, finely sliced
- 400g can chopped tomatoes
- 400g can chickpeas, rinsed and drained
- 4 cups reduced salt fish stock
- 500g firm white fish fillets (redfish, bream, sea perch), cut into large pieces
- 1/3 cup couscous
- thick, low-fat plain yoghurt, to serve
- 1 tbsp chopped fresh parsley
- 1 tbsp chopped fresh mint
- Lebanese bread, to serve

1. Heat the oil in a stockpot, add the onion and cook over a medium heat for 3 minutes or until the onion is soft and golden.
2. Add the spices and chilli and cook until fragrant (about 2 minutes). Stir in the tomatoes, chickpeas and fish stock and bring to the boil. Reduce the heat and simmer uncovered for 15 minutes.
3. Add the fish and cook for 5 minutes or just until the fish is tender. Remove the soup from the heat then add the couscous and cover. Set aside for 10 minutes or until the couscous is soft.
4. Serve with a dollop of yoghurt and sprinkled with parsley and mint. Accompany with wedges of Lebanese bread.

Serves 6

PRAWN AND CHICKEN SOUP

Preparation 15 mins **Cooking** 15 mins **Calories** 209 **Fat** trace

1 tbsp vegetable oil
1 onion, diced
1 red capsicum, diced
2 cloves garlic, crushed
1 tsp finely chopped fresh ginger
4 cups chicken stock
125g boneless chicken thigh or breast, fillets, sliced
20 uncooked small prawns, shelled and deveined
125g rice noodles
125g canned bamboo shoots, drained and sliced
5 white mushrooms, thinly sliced
$^{1}/_{4}$ lettuce, shredded
2 green onions, thinly sliced
2 tbsps finely chopped fresh coriander
$1^{1}/_{2}$ tbsps soy sauce
freshly ground black pepper

1. Heat oil in a stockpot over a medium heat, add onion and red capsicum and cook, stirring, for 5 minutes or until onion is soft. Add garlic and ginger and cook for 2 minutes longer.
2. Stir in stock and bring to the boil. Add chicken, prawns, noodles, bamboo shoots and mushrooms, reduce heat and simmer for 5 minutes or until noodles are tender.
3. Stir in lettuce, green onions, coriander, soy sauce and black pepper to taste, and serve immediately.

Serves 4

CHILLI KUMARA SOUP

Preparation 15 mins **Cooking** 25 mins **Calories** 35 **Fat** 2g

- 6 cups chicken stock
- 3 stalks fresh lemongrass, bruised or $1\frac{1}{2}$ tsps dried lemongrass, soaked in hot water until soft
- 3 fresh red chillies, halved
- 10 slices fresh or bottled galangal or fresh ginger
- 5–6 fresh coriander plants, roots washed, leaves removed and reserved
- 1 large kumara (orange sweet potato), peeled and cut into 2cm pieces
- $\frac{3}{4}$ cup coconut cream
- 1 tbsp Thai fish sauce (nam pla)

1. Place stock, lemongrass, chillies, galangal or ginger and coriander roots in a stockpot and bring to the boil over a medium heat. Add kumara (sweet potato) and simmer, uncovered, for 15 minutes or until kumara is soft.
2. Remove lemongrass, galangal or ginger and coriander roots and discard. Cool liquid slightly, then purée soup, in batches, in a food processor or blender. Return soup to a clean stockpot and stir in 125mL of the coconut cream and the fish sauce. Cook, stirring, over a medium heat for 4 minutes or until heated. Stir in $\frac{2}{3}$ of the reserved coriander leaves.
3. To serve, ladle soup into bowls, top with a little of the remaining coconut cream and scatter with remaining coriander leaves.

Serves 4

CLASSIC BOUILLABAISSE

Preparation 10 mins **Cooking** 2 hrs 15 mins **Calories** 341 **Fat** 3g

Stock

- 3 kg fish heads and bones
- 4 tbsps olive oil
- 3 cups dry white wine
- 4 carrots, peeled and sliced
- 2 leeks, washed and sliced
- 2 onions, peeled and sliced
- 3 sticks celery
- 6 tomatoes, chopped
- 1 tsp peppercorns
- 1 bunch thyme, tied together, rinsed
- 1 bunch parsley, tied together
- 1 bunch dill, tied together
- 4 fresh bay leaves
- 12 cups of water

Soup

- 2 tbsps olive oil
- 2 large leeks
- 1 large fennel bulb, finely sliced
- 6 shallots, peeled and sliced
- 3 medium potatoes, peeled and diced
- large pinch of saffron threads
- 2 x 400g cans Italian style tomatoes
- 2 kg assorted fish fillets, diced
- 600g large prawns, peeled
- 1 kg mussels, scrubbed and rinsed
- 500g small squid, cleaned
- 1/2 bunch parsley, chopped
- 1 loaf sourdough bread
- salt and pepper, to taste

Rouille

- 1/2 cup breadcrumbs
- 1/4 cup liquid from the soup
- 2 large red capsicums
- 2 small, red chillies
- 3 cloves garlic
- 1 tsp red wine vinegar
- salt and pepper, to taste
- olive oil

Stock

1 Rinse the heads and bones and set aside. Heat the olive oil in a deep stockpot, then add the fish heads and bones. Cook the fish over a high heat, stirring constantly, until the fish pieces begin to break down, scraping up anything that sticks to the bottom of the pan (about 20 minutes). Add the wine and simmer, stirring well. Add the prepared vegetables, herbs, bay leaves and water and simmer for 30 minutes, skimming any scum off the surface as it appears. After 30 minutes, strain the stock thoroughly, pressing on the solids to extract as much liquid as possible. Return to the heat for a further 20 minutes, then add salt and pepper to taste. Set aside.

Soup

1 Heat the olive oil and add the sliced leeks, fennel, shallots, potatoes and saffron and cook over a medium heat until all the vegetables are golden and soft (about 20 minutes). Add the squashed canned tomatoes and reserved fish stock and bring the soup to the boil. Add salt and pepper to taste.

2 Add the fish, prawns and mussels and simmer for 10 minutes. Add the cleaned squid and parsley and stir gently. Remove the soup from the heat and cover. Allow to rest for 10 minutes. Meanwhile, brush the sliced sourdough bread with olive oil and grill until golden on both sides. Rub a clove of garlic over each golden slice. To serve, place a slice of grilled bread on the bottom of each soup bowl and ladle the hot soup over the top, making sure that everyone gets some mussels, prawns and squid. Add a spoonful of rouille if desired.-

Rouille

1 First, cut the sides off the capsicums and roast the capsicum slices by placing them, skin side up, under a hot grill until blistered. Place the capsicum pieces in a plastic bag until cool then peel and discard the skin. Chop all the ingredients except the olive oil, in a food processor, taking care not to over process. When the ingredients are well mixed add enough olive oil and salt and pepper to taste to make a flavoursome paste.

Serves 4

Note: This soup is traditionally garnished with a rouille, a type of paste made from red capsicums and a hint of chilli.

CRAB SOUP

Preparation 20 mins **Cooking** 5 mins **Calories** 73 **Fat** trace

- 170g can crabmeat (or fresh, picked crabmeat)
- 1 egg
- 4 dried Chinese mushrooms
- 85g canned bamboo shoots
- 1 leek
- small piece fresh ginger
- 1 tbsp vegetable oil
- 2 tbsps soy sauce
- 1 tbsp rice wine, mirin or dry sherry
- 6 cups fish or chicken stock
- 2 tsps salt
- freshly ground pepper
- 1 1/2 tbsps cornflour
- 2 tbsps parsley, chopped

1. Drain crabmeat and break up. Beat the egg in a small bowl. Soak dried mushrooms in water for 20 minutes, discard stalks, then slice caps. Drain bamboo shoots and cut them into strips, slit the leek almost through, discarding tough green, wash carefully, then cut into strips. Grate or finely chop ginger.
2. Heat the oil in a wok or medium stockpot, add the mushrooms, leek, bamboo shoots and ginger and stir- fry for 1 minute.
3. Add the crabmeat, sprinkle with soy sauce, rice wine and pour in the heated stock or water. As soon as the liquid comes to the boil, skim off any scum. Season with salt and pepper, stir in the cornflour mixed with a little water, to thicken the soup.
4. Pour in the beaten egg and mix, stirring lightly so that the egg sets in short strands. Sprinkle with finely chopped parsley and serve.

Serves 4–6

CLAM CHOWDER

Preparation 8 mins **Cooking** 27 mins **Calories** 1070 **Fat** 32g

1 kg clam meat
250g butter
6 rashers bacon, finely chopped
3 onions, finely chopped
$1^1/_2$ cups celery, finely chopped
1 cup plain flour
5 cups milk
3 cups fish stock
10 tbsp parsley, freshly chopped
salt and pepper, to taste
5 cups boiled potatoes, finely diced

1. Melt butter, add the bacon, onion and celery into the pot and cook until tender (about 5 minutes).
2. Add the flour and cook for 2 minutes.
3. Add the milk, fish stock and potatoes, cover and simmer for 10 minutes.
4. Add the clam meat and cook again for 10 minutes. Season to taste.
5. Serve in a deep plate with cream and parsley.

Serves 4

Note: Extra vegetables of your choice may be added – it is a good way to use up vegetable leftovers.

CREAMY OYSTER BISQUE

Preparation 15 mins + blending **Cooking** 25 mins **Calories** 239 **Fat** 2g

- 20 fresh oysters, shucked, or 1 jar of about 20 oysters, drained and liquid reserved
- 4 cups reduced salt fish or vegetable stock
- 1/2 cup white wine
- 1 small white onion or 1/2 leek, diced
- 1 stalk celery, diced
- 2 cups diced peeled potato
- 1 tbsp fresh thyme, chopped or 1 tsp dried thyme
- 1/2 cup low-fat milk
- freshly ground black pepper, to taste
- sprigs watercress or fresh parsley, optional

1. Measure the liquid from the oysters. Add stock to the liquid from the oysters to make up a total of 1 cup.
2. Heat 2 tablespoons of the wine in a large stockpot over a low heat. Add onion and celery. Cook, stirring, for 4–5 minutes or until onion is transparent. Add potato and thyme. Stir in the stock mixture and the remaining wine. Bring to simmering. Simmer for 10–15 minutes or until the potatoes are soft and most of the liquid is absorbed. Cool slightly.
3. Transfer mixture to a food processor or blender. Add half the oysters, the milk and black pepper to taste. Purée. Return the mixture to a clean stockpot. Bring to the boil. Remove the soup from the heat. Stir in the remaining oysters.
4. To serve, ladle soup into warm bowls and top with watercress or parsley sprigs, if desired.

Serves 4

LOBSTER BISQUE

Preparation 10 mins + purée **Cooking** 35 mins **Calories** 320 **Fat** 13g

- 1 small lobster, cooked
- 1 large carrot, peeled and diced
- 1 small onion, finely chopped
- 125g butter
- $^3/_4$ cup dry white wine
- bouquet garni
- $6^1/_2$ cups fish or chicken stock
- $^1/_3$ - $^3/_4$ cup rice
- salt, pepper and ground cayenne, to taste
- $^1/_2$ cup cream
- 2 tbsps brandy
- parsley, chopped

1. Split the lobster in half, lengthwise, and remove the flesh from the shell, then set it aside. Wrap the shell in an old tea towel, crush the shell with a hammer and set aside. Sauté the carrot and onion in half the butter until softened without colouring (about 5 minutes). Add the crushed shell, sauté a further minute or so then add the wine. Boil hard until reduced by half. Add the bouquet garni, stock and the rice.
2. After about 20 minutes, when the rice is tender, remove the large pieces of shell and the bouquet garni. Purée in a food processor with the remainder of the batter, doing so in small batches. Pour through a strainer. Rinse out the food processor to remove every trace of shell and purée the strained liquid again, this time with the lobster flesh, saving a few pieces for the garnish. Reheat gently.
3. Add salt, pepper and cayenne to taste, then stir in the cream, brandy and reserved lobster pieces cut into thin slices. Serve very hot, garnished with parsley.

Serves 6

MALTESE MUSSELS

Preparation 20 mins **Cooking** 40 mins **Calories** 301 **Fat** 3g

500g black mussels, cleaned
2 roasted capsicums, peeled and diced
3 garlic cloves, chopped
1 orange, juice and grated zest
$^{1}/_{2}$ fennel bulb, diced
$^{1}/_{2}$ celery stick, diced
$^{3}/_{5}$ cup white wine
$^{4}/_{5}$ cup tomato juice
salt, pepper, cayenne pepper, and paprika, to taste
2 cups chicken stock
$^{2}/_{5}$ cup olive oil

1. In a large stockpot on medium heat, add oil, onion, garlic, capsicum, tomato, fennel, celery and cook for 10 minutes.
2. Add white wine, orange juice, zest, tomato juice, chicken stock, seasoning and cook for 20 minutes.
3. Add mussels and cook until all mussels have opened, about 8–10 minutes. Discard any mussels that do not open.
4. Serve with wood-fired bread or Grissini.

Serves 4

MUSSELS WITH WITLOF AND BASIL SOUP

Preparation 15 mins **Cooking** 15 mins **Calories** 254 **Fat** 9g

30g butter

2 witlof or Belgian endives, with leaves cut loose

1 cup broth from cooking the mussels, strained

2 tbsps double cream

15 basil leaves, chopped finely

salt and pepper

1 kg black mussels cleaned, cooked Mariniére style and removed from shell

Mussels Mariniére Style

1 small onion, sliced

1 stick celery, sliced

1 clove garlic, chopped

55mL white wine

pepper, to taste

1 tbsp butter

1 tbsp parsley, chopped

1 Melt butter in a pot and stir-fry witlofs.

2 Add broth, cream and basil, mix well with a whisk until ingredients all blend in together.

3 Add mussels, heat until boiling and serve in bowls.

Mussels Mariniére Style

1 Place the mussels, onion, celery, garlic and white wine in a large stockpot.

2 Cook over a medium heat until the mussels have opened. Stir frequently to ensure that the mussels cook evenly.

3 Add pepper to taste. Stir in the butter and pepper just before serving.

Serves 4

MUSSEL SOUP

Preparation 20 mins **Cooking** 15 mins **Calories** 436 **Fat** 16g

- $1^{1}/_{5}$ cups water
- 1 small carrot, diced finely
- 55g cauliflower, divided into florets
- $^{1}/_{2}$ red capsicum, diced finely
- $^{1}/_{2}$ onion, diced finely
- 1 pinch saffron
- 10 coriander seeds, cracked
- 45mL sherry vinegar
- 85g butter
- 2 tbsps plain flour
- 1 kg black mussels, cooked as Mariniére style (see page 37)
- 2 tbsps double cream
- salt and pepper, to taste
- 1 tbsp fresh parsley, finely chopped

1. In a large stockpot on a high heat combine water, carrot, cauliflower, capsicum, onion, saffron and coriander seeds.
2. Bring to the boil and add the vinegar. Remove from heat and allow to cool down.
3. When cold, strain the vegetables from the cooking liquid.
4. In a cooking pot on a medium heat, melt the butter then add the flour. Stir with a wooden spoon and cook gently for 2 minutes.
5. Add the broth slowly with a whisk and cook until slightly thickened, with a smooth consistency.
6. Add reserved vegetables, mussels, cream and bring to the boil. Taste and season if necessary with salt and pepper. Add parsley just before serving.

Serves 4

PIPI AND BLACK MUSSEL BROTH

Preparation 15 mins **Cooking** 10 mins **Calories** 239 **Fat** 2g

- 200g pipies, cleaned of sand
- 200g black mussels, cleaned
- 1 onion, finely chopped
- 1 stalk lemongrass, chopped
- juice of 1 lime
- 2 tbsps Tom Yum paste
- 3 cups chicken stock
- 1 tbsp fresh coriander leaves, roughly chopped
- 1 tbsp coriander stalk and roots, finely chopped
- 1 tbsp Thai fish sauce (nam pla)
- 55mL vegetable oil

1. In a wok or the Baccarat stockpot, on a high heat, add oil, onions, Tom Yum paste, pipies and mussels, and simmer with a lid on for 30 seconds.
2. Add chicken stock, lemongrass, lime juice, coriander stalk and roots, Thai fish sauce and stir through; cook until all shells have opened.
3. Add fresh coriander leaves and serve in soup bowls.

Serves 4

RUSTIC MEDITERRANEAN SEAFOOD SOUP

Preparation 20 mins **Cooking** 30 mins **Calories** 234 **Fat** trace

- 200g calamari tubes, cleaned
- 285g green prawns
- 200g mussels
- 250g mixed firm white fish fillets (red mullet, sea perch, red fish)
- 1 tbsp olive oil
- 2 cloves garlic, crushed
- 1 onion, finely chopped
- 1/2 cup white wine
- 400g can tomatoes, chopped
- 3 cups reduced salt fish stock
- pinch saffron
- 2 potatoes (about 285g), peeled and cut into large cubes

1. Cut the calamari tubes into rings. Peel and devein the prawns, leaving the tails intact. Scrub the mussels and remove their hairy beards. Discard any mussels that are already open. Remove any bones from the fish and cut it into large pieces.
2. Heat the oil in a large stockpot. Add the garlic and onion and cook over a medium heat for 3 minutes or until the onion is golden. Add the white wine and bring to the boil. Cook over a high heat until nearly all the liquid has been absorbed.
3. Add the tomatoes, fish stock, saffron and potatoes and simmer for 15 minutes or until the potatoes are tender. Do not overcook or they will start to break up.
4. Add all the seafood and simmer for 3–5 minutes or until tender. Serve with crusty Italian bread.

Serves 6

THAI PRAWN SOUP WITH LEMONGRASS

Preparation 15 mins **Cooking** 15 mins **Calories** 43 **Fat** trace

- 125g large green prawns
- 3 stalks lemongrass
- 4 cups reduced salt fish stock
- 2cm piece ginger, peeled and cut into fine strips
- 2 kaffir lime leaves
- 1/2 small pineapple, peeled and cored
- 1 tbsp fish sauce
- 1 tbsp lime juice
- 6 green onions, thinly sliced on the diagonal
- 1/2 cup fresh coriander leaves
- pepper, to taste

1 Peel and devein the prawns, leaving the tails intact. Reserve the shells and discard the veins. Halve the lemongrass stalks and squash the bases with the flat side of a knife.

2 Place the prawn shells in a medium stockpot with the stock and bring slowly to the boil. Reduce the heat and simmer gently
for 10 minutes. Strain, then return to the pot and add the lemongrass, ginger and lime leaves, and return to simmering point.

3 Cut the pineapple into thin pieces and add to the stock along with the prawns, and simmer just until the prawns turn pink and tender (a few minutes, depending on their size). Add the fish sauce, lime juice, green onions and coriander.

4 Remove the lemongrass and lime leaves, season with pepper and serve immediately.

Serves 6

FAMILY FAVOURITES

THERE IS NOTHING QUITE LIKE THE DELICIOUS AROMA OF HOME-MADE SOUP WAFTING THROUGH YOUR HOME. THE ONLY THING THAT COMES CLOSE IS THE SATISFACTION YOU FEEL WHEN YOU HAVE MADE A SENSATIONAL SOUP ALL BY YOURSELF! THE ONLY DIFFICULT THING ABOUT THESE RECIPES IS DECIDING WHICH ONE TO COOK FIRST.

CARIBBEAN GAZPACHO WITH AVOCADO SALSA

Preparation 12 mins + refrigeration **Cooking** none **Calories** 149 **Fat** trace

- $^{1}/_{2}$ cup cucumber, finely diced
- $^{1}/_{2}$ cup pineapple, finely diced
- $^{1}/_{2}$ cup mango, finely diced
- $^{1}/_{4}$ red capsicum, finely diced
- 2 Roma tomatoes, finely diced
- 1 green onion, chopped
- 2 tbsps mint, freshly chopped
- 2 tbsps coriander, freshly chopped
- 1 cup tomato or vegetable juice
- 1 cup pineapple juice
- 1 tsp no-added-salt Worcestershire sauce
- tabasco sauce

Avocado Salsa

- 1 avocado, diced
- 1 tbsp coriander, freshly chopped
- 1 tsp lime juice

1 Place the cucumber, pineapple, mango, red capsicum, tomatoes, green onion, mint, coriander, tomato and pineapple juices, Worcestershire sauce and tabasco sauce to taste in a glass bowl. Mix to combine. Cover. Refrigerate overnight or until cold.

2 To serve, ladle the soup into chilled bowls. Top with a spoonful of salsa.

Avocado Salsa

1 Place the avocado, coriander and lime juice in a bowl. Mix to combine. Cover. Refrigerate until ready to use. The salsa is best used within a few days of being made.

Serves 4

YELLOW CAPSICUM SOUP WITH RED CAPSICUM HARISSA

Preparation 15 mins **Cooking** 30 mins **Calories** 174 **Fat** trace

- 2 tsps olive oil
- 3 yellow capsicums, diced
- 1 carrot, finely diced
- 1 small onion, diced
- 1 cup potato, diced
- 2 cups hot reduced salt vegetable or chicken stock
- 2 tsp orange zest, grated
- juice of 1 orange

Red Capsicum Harissa

- 2 red capsicums, cut in half lengthwise, seeds removed
- 1 Roma tomato, cut in half lengthwise, seeds removed
- 1 tbsp red wine vinegar
- 2 tsps no-added-salt tomato paste
- hot chilli sauce
- freshly ground black pepper, to taste

1. Heat the oil in a large non-stick frypan over a low heat. Add the yellow capsicums, carrot and onion. Cook, stirring, for 10 minutes or until the peppers are soft. Add the potato and stock. Bring to simmering. Simmer for 20 minutes or until the potato is soft. Cool slightly.
2. Transfer mixture to a food processor. Add orange zest and juice. Purée. Season with black pepper to taste. Return soup to a clean stockpot. Reheat.
3. To serve, ladle soup into warm bowls. Top with harissa.

Harissa

1. Preheat grill to hot. Using your hands, gently flatten the red capsicum and tomato halves and place, skin side up, on aluminium foil under the grill. Cook until skins blacken. Set aside until cool enough to handle. Remove skins.
2. Place pepper and tomato flesh in a food processor. Add vinegar, tomato paste and hot chilli sauce and black pepper to taste. Purée. Set aside until ready to serve.

Serves 4

SORREL SOUP

Preparation 8 mins **Cooking** 30 mins **Calories** 206 **Fat** 8g

30g butter
2 leeks, finely sliced
4 medium potatoes, diced
6 cups chicken stock
salt and freshly ground black pepper, to taste
6–8 sorrel or young spinach leaves, shredded and mixed with 1 tsp lemon juice

1 Melt the butter in a large stockpot and cook the leeks over low heat until soft. Add the potatoes and stock and bring to the boil. Lower the heat and simmer gently for 20 minutes or until potatoes are tender. Season to taste with salt and black pepper. Add the sorrel or spinach to the soup, bring to the boil and serve.

Serves 6

TOMATO AND MEATBALL SOUP

Preparation 10 mins **Cooking** 7 mins **Calories** 155 **Fat** 4g

1 egg, beaten
1 tbsp soy sauce
1 tbsp sherry
1 tbsp onion, chopped
$^{1}/_{2}$ tsp fresh ginger, finely grated
250g lean minced pork or beef
2 tbsps cornflour
4 cups beef stock
1 leek, finely sliced
4 firm, ripe tomatoes, peeled, seeded and diced
chopped fresh coriander or green onions for garnish (optional)

1 Combine the egg, soy sauce, sherry, onion and ginger in a bowl, add the meat and cornflour, then mix well and set aside.

2 Place the stock in a large stockpot, add the leek and tomatoes and bring to the boil. Boil for 2–3 minutes, then lower the heat.

3 Drop rounded teaspoonfuls of the meat mixture into the soup, cover and gently simmer for 3–4 minutes or until meatballs are cooked. Serve sprinkled with coriander or green onions.

Serves 4–6

MUSHROOM AND ONION CONSOMME

Preparation 10 mins **Cooking** 1 1/2 hrs **Calories** 81 **Fat** 1g

1 kg mushrooms, roughly chopped
1 kg onions, chopped
8 cups water
1 tsp salt
1 tbsp fresh lemon juice
55mL Madeira or dry sherry
freshly ground black pepper, to taste

Garnish
spring onion, thin julienne strips
white mushrooms, finely sliced
radish, finely sliced
6–8 sprigs fresh watercress

1 Place the mushrooms and onions in a large stockpot. Add the water, salt and lemon juice and bring slowly to the boil. Lower the heat, cover and simmer gently for 1 1/2 hours.

2 Strain the liquid through a fine sieve and return to a clean stockpot. Add Madeira or sherry and season to taste with black pepper. Heat through and serve with garnishes.

Serves 6–8

BORSCH WITH CUCUMBER YOGHURT

Preparation 15 mins **Cooking** 50 mins **Calories** 137 **Fat** trace

1 tbsp olive oil
1 onion, thinly sliced
1 clove garlic, crushed
1cm piece fresh ginger, grated
1 tbsp no-added-salt tomato paste
3 large beets, thinly sliced
1 large potato, thinly sliced
1 parsnip, thinly sliced
1 bay leaf
6 cups reduced salt chicken or vegetable stock
2 tbsps red wine vinegar
juice of 1 lemon or orange
freshly ground black pepper

Cucumber Yoghurt

1/2 bunch fresh chives
1/4 cup cucumber, finely diced
1 tbsp fresh dill, chopped
1 tsp lemon juice
1 cup thick low-fat plain yoghurt

1. Heat the oil in a large stockpot over a medium heat. Add the onion, garlic and ginger. Cook, stirring, for 5 minutes or until ingredients are soft.
2. Stir in the tomato paste. Cook for 1–2 minutes. Add the beets, potato and parsnip. Cook, stirring, for 2–3 minutes. Add the bay leaf, stock, vinegar and lemon juice. Bring to the boil, then reduce heat. Cover. Simmer for 30–40 minutes or until vegetables are soft. Season with black pepper to taste. Cool slightly.
3. Transfer mixture to a food processor or blender, and purée in batches. Return the soup to a clean stockpot. Bring back to the boil. Check seasoning. Add more lemon juice if necessary.
4. To serve, ladle soup into warm bowls. Top with a spoonful of the cucumber yoghurt.

Cucumber Yoghurt

1. Bring a stockpot of water to the boil. Blanch the chives. Drain well. Place the chives in a food processor. Add the cucumber, dill and lemon juice, and process to make a paste. Transfer mixture to a bowl. Stir in yoghurt. Cover. Refrigerate until ready to use.

Serves 6

COUNTRY VEGETABLE SOUP WITH BASIL

Preparation 10 mins + soaking **Cooking** 1 hrs 30 mins **Calories** 574 **Fat** 6g

500g dried haricot beans
1 large onion
500g green beans
500g zucchini
5 medium potatoes
30g butter
2–3 rashers bacon
8–10 cups water
2 tsps salt

Basil Paste

1 cup basil leaves, finely shredded
4 cloves garlic, crushed
2 ripe tomatoes, peeled and chopped
1 tbsp tomato paste
1/2 cup cheese, finely grated
3 tbsps olive oil

1. Soak the beans overnight or for several hours. Place them in a large pan with fresh water to cover. Bring to the boil, cover and simmer for 20 minutes, then drain. Meanwhile, chop the onion finely. Trim the green beans and cut them into short lengths. Cut zucchini into fairly thick slices. Peel potatoes and dice.
2. Melt the butter in the stockpot and sauté the bacon and prepared vegetables, including the haricot beans, until softened, (about 5 minutes). Cover with cold water and add salt. Cover with a lid and simmer gently for 1 hour.
3. Meanwhile, make basil paste and stir into soup just before serving. Serve hot with cheese toasts or crusty bread.

Basil Paste

1. Combine basil leaves and garlic in a bowl. Add the tomatoes to the basil with tomato paste and cheese. Pound this mixture in a blender or food processor to make a smooth paste. Gradually beat in olive oil. Set aside to serve with soup.

Serves 4–6

SWEET POTATO, PASTA AND LEEK SOUP

Preparation 20 mins **Cooking** 40 mins **Calories** 344 **Fat** 7g

- 2 tsps canola oil
- 2 leeks, thinly sliced
- pinch saffron
- 1 kg sweet potato, peeled and chopped
- 8 cups reduced salt chicken stock
- 1 cinnamon stick
- 1 bouquet garni
- 125g ditalini (tiny pasta pieces for soup)
- 2 tbsps fresh chives, chopped

Lavash Crisps

- 2 sheets lavash bread
- 1 tbsp olive oil
- 2 tbsps Parmesan cheese, finely grated

1. Heat the oil in a large stockpot, add the leeks and cook over a medium heat for 5 minutes or until the leeks are soft and golden. Add the saffron and sweet potato and stir for about 5 minutes or until the sweet potato begins to soften.
2. Stir in the stock, cinnamon stick and bouquet garni. Bring to the boil then reduce the heat and simmer for 30 minutes, or until the sweet potato is very soft. Remove the cinnamon stick and bouquet garni.
3. Cook the pasta in a large stockpot of rapidly boiling water until al dente (cooked, but still with a bite to it). Drain well.
4. Purée the soup in batches until smooth, then return to the pot along with the pasta and reheat gently. If it is too thick add a little water.

Lavash Crisps

1. Use a star-shaped cookie cutter to cut out shapes from the bread, brush lightly with oil, sprinkle with parmesan cheese and place another star on top. Grill until crisp and golden.
2. To serve, ladle the soup into bowls, float lavash stars on top and sprinkle with chives.

Serves 6

CHUNKY FRESH TOMATO SOUP

Preparation 12 mins **Cooking** 10 mins **Calories** 39 **Fat** trace

- 4 ripe tomatoes
- 1 tbsp olive oil
- 1 clove garlic, crushed
- 2 tbsps fresh herbs (parsley, basil or combination)
- pinch of sugar
- $2^1/2$ cups chicken stock
- salt and freshly ground pepper, to taste

1. Peel the tomatoes by holding them over a gas flame for 30 seconds, then the skins will easily slip off, or cover them with boiling water, count to 10, then plunge them into cold water and remove the skin. Cut the blossom end from the tomatoes, halve them and flip out the seeds, then chop.
2. Heat the oil and add the tomatoes, garlic and 1 tablespoon of the chopped herbs. Add a pinch of sugar and cook gently for 5 minutes, then add the stock and cook for a further 5 minutes. Taste and adjust seasoning.
3. Serve immediately, sprinkled with the remaining herbs to garnish and croutons or crostini (slim bread sticks). Or cool, place in the refrigerator and serve chilled.

Serves 6

CREAM OF HARICOT BEAN SOUP WITH KRANSKY AND CAPSICUM

Preparation 10 mins + soaking **Cooking** 1 hr **Calories** 345 **Fat** 10g

125g haricot beans, soaked overnight
55g butter
3 medium onions, finely chopped
3 carrots, scrubbed and diced
3 cloves garlic, crushed
5 cups chicken stock
bouquet garni
2 green capsicums
1 tbsp olive oil
250g poached kransky or other smoked sausage
salt and freshly ground pepper

1. Melt the butter in a large stockpot and gently sauté the onions, carrots and garlic until soft and just beginning to colour.
2. Add the stock and bouquet garni. Drain the beans and add them to the pan. Bring slowly to the boil, reduce heat and simmer gently, half covered, until beans are very tender, for about 1 hour.
3. In several lots, transfer the soup to a food processor or blender and process until smooth. Return puréed soup to the pan and reheat gently. If the soup is too thick, add a little water or the stock. Check for seasoning with salt and pepper.
4. Meanwhile, cut capsicums into small dice and pan fry in olive oil until tender and still a little crisp. Carefully peel the skin from the sausage and cut it into small dice.
5. Ladle the soup into heated bowls and sprinkle each generously with the capsicums and the sausage.

Serves 6

CREAM OF BROCCOLI SOUP

Preparation 15 mins **Cooking** 15 mins **Calories** 177 **Fat** 4g

2 potatoes, peeled
1 large carrot, sliced
1 head broccoli
4 cups chicken stock
$^{1}/_{3}$ cup milk
30g butter
salt and pepper
pinch grated nutmeg
2 egg yolks
$^{1}/_{4}$ cup cream

1. Place the potatoes and carrot in a large stockpot of boiling salted water. Remove the thick woody stalks from the broccoli and break it into florets. Drop broccoli into water with potatoes and carrots and cook until tender (about 10 minutes). Drain and press through a sieve or purée in a blender or food processor. Put in a pan, add stock and bring it slowly to the boil. Add the milk, butter and seasonings.
2. Combine the egg yolks with the cream and a little of the hot soup. Blend well and return to the pan. Without boiling, cook gently until the soup thickens. If you like, offer croutons or croutes of bread fried to a gold crisp in olive oil, when serving.

Serves 6

SPINACH AND NUTMEG SOUP WITH CHEESE TOASTS

Preparation 20 mins + 10 mins cooling **Cooking** 25 mins **Calories** 298 **Fat** 19g

2 tbsps olive oil
30g butter
250g floury potatoes, peeled and cut into $2^1/2$cm cubes
250g spinach leaves
1 tsp nutmeg, freshly grated
6 cups chicken or vegetable stock
salt and black pepper

Cheese Toasts

4 tbsps crème fraîche
100g Gruyère, Caerphilly or Cheddar cheese, grated
1 large egg, beaten
day-old narrow French bread stick, cut diagonally into 18 x 1cm slices

1 Heat the oil and half the butter in a large stockpot. Fry the potatoes for 1 minute, then add the spinach and the nutmeg. Cook for 2 minutes or until the spinach is wilting.

2 Add the stock to the potato and spinach mixture, season lightly and bring to the boil. Reduce the heat, cover and simmer for 10–15 minutes, until the potatoes are tender. Leave to cool for 10 minutes.

3 Pour the soup into a food processor and blend until smooth, or use a hand blender. Stir in half the crème fraîche, then adjust the seasoning to taste. Set aside.

Cheese Toasts

1 Preheat the grill. Mix the grated cheese with the egg and the rest of the crème fraîche. Lightly toast the bread slices, then spread the cheese mixture over one side of each slice. Dot with the rest of the butter and season with a little black pepper. Grill for 5 minutes or until bubbling and golden. Heat the soup through and serve topped with the cheese toasts.

Serves 6

Note: Little toasts covered with cheese and a dash of crème fraîche make a great topping for spinach soup, which can be made in advance and heated through before serving.

CHICKEN VEGETABLE SOUP WITH CHEESE STICKS

Preparation 30 mins **Cooking** 40 mins **Calories** 426 **Fat** 22g

2 skinless chicken breast fillets
4 cups reduced salt chicken stock
1 tbsp canola oil
2 leeks, washed and thinly sliced
2 carrots, diced
2 sticks celery, diced
3 cloves garlic, crushed
6 cups young green leaves (watercress, rocket, sorrel, baby spinach), washed
3 tbsps fresh pesto
cracked black pepper, to taste

Cheese Sticks

1 sheet canola puff pastry, thawed
3 tbsps reduced fat cheese, finely grated

1. Put the chicken in a pot, add just enough chicken stock to cover it and poach gently for about 10 minutes or until just cooked. Set aside to cool.
2. Heat the oil in a large pot, add the leeks and cook gently for about 2 minutes until soft. Add the carrot, celery and garlic, strain the chicken poaching stock through a fine sieve and
   add to the vegetables with the rest of the stock. Simmer for 10 minutes. Chop the greens finely, add them to the soup and cook for a further 10 minutes.
3. Tear the chicken breasts into fine shreds and add them to the soup. Stir in the pesto and season with plenty of cracked black pepper.

Cheese Sticks

1. Preheat oven. Cut the puff pastry into 2cm thick strips and place on a baking tray lined with baking parchment. Sprinkle with the cheese and bake for 20 minutes or until crisp and golden.
2. Serve the soup in wide bowls with cheese sticks.

Serves 6

Oven temperature 220°C, 440°F,Gas 7

COUNTRY-STYLE GREEN SOUP

Preparation 10 mins **Cooking** 30 mins **Calories** 274 **Fat** 13g

- 500g spinach or silverbeet, stems discarded
- 10–12 fresh sorrel leaves
- 45g butter
- 1 small onion, finely chopped
- 340g potatoes, peeled and sliced
- 5 cups chicken stock
- salt and freshly ground black pepper, to taste
- freshly grated nutmeg, to taste
- 2 tbsps fresh parsley, chopped
- 1 egg yolk
- 1 cup double cream
- extra double cream and snipped fresh chives, to garnish

1. Wash and dry the spinach and sorrel on paper towels, roughly chop them, then blend or process until well ground. Set aside.
2. Heat the butter in a stockpot, add the onion and cook over a moderate heat, stirring, until soft. Add the potatoes and stir until the potatoes are well coated with butter. Add the stock and bring to the boil.
3. Lower the heat and simmer, partially covered, for 15 minutes or until the potatoes are tender. Remove from the heat, season to taste with salt, black pepper and nutmeg and cool slightly.
4. Purée the mixture with ground greens and parsley, in batches, in a blender or food processor. Return to a clean stockpot and bring to simmering.
5. Mix the egg yolk with the cream in a bowl, stir in a little of the hot soup, then return the mixture to the stockpot. Heat through without boiling. Serve in heated bowls with a swirl of extra cream and a few chives.

Serves 6

ASIAN DELIGHTS

THE SENSATIONAL FLAVOURS AND AROMAS FOR WHICH ASIAN FOOD IS RENOWN FIND NEW LIFE IN THESE DELICIOUS SOUPS. TRY THEM FOR A WARMING MEAL, OR AS A STARTER FOR AN ASIAN FEAST – THESE RECIPES CONTAIN SOMETHING PERFECT FOR EVERY OCCASION.

JAPANESE SPRING ONION, SESAME AND SHIITAKE SOUP

Preparation 10 mins + resting **Cooking** 10 mins **Calories** 73 **Fat** trace

- 55g dried shiitake mushrooms
- 4 cups chicken stock
- 2 cups beef stock
- 30g piece of fresh ginger, sliced
- 1 tsp toasted sesame oil
- 1/2 tsp five spice powder
- 1 tbsp teriyaki sauce*
- 2 tbsps mirin*
- 125g white mushrooms, finely sliced
- 6 spring onions, sliced diagonally
- 1 tbsp sesame seeds

1. Heat the chicken and beef stocks in a stockpot and add the shiitake mushrooms and sliced ginger. Bring the stocks to the boil, then simmer for 5 minutes. Remove from the heat and allow to rest for 40 minutes.
2. Remove the mushrooms from the liquid and carefully slice them, discarding stems. Remove the ginger from the stock and set aside. Line a sieve with some paper towel then pour the stock into the sieve. Allow the stock to drain through the sieve, straining out all the grit and sand from the mushrooms. Discard the paper.
3. Return the strained stock, ginger and shittake mushrooms to the stockpot and bring it to a simmer. Add the sesame oil, five spice powder, teriyaki sauce, mirin and finely sliced white mushrooms and simmer for 10 minutes.
4. Remove the ginger then add the sliced spring onions.
5. Serve the soup in Japanese bowls, garnished with the sesame seeds.

Serves 6

Note: This simple soup is light and refreshing yet full of intense, Asian overtones. It is perfect served before a main course of stir-fried beef and vegetables with teriyaki sauce. If you want a simpler meal, just accompany this delicious soup with a bowl of perfectly steamed rice.

*Available from Asian food stores

FISH NOODLE SOUP

Preparation 10 mins **Cooking** 10 mins **Calories** 261 **Fat** 6g

500g white fish fillets
vegetable oil
85g green onions
1 tsp fresh ginger, chopped,
1 tsp garlic, chopped or crushed
1 red capsicum, seeded and chopped
4 cups fish stock or water
1 tbsp oyster sauce
$^{1}/_{2}$ tsp ground black pepper
1 tsp sesame oil
1 tbsp dry sherry
250g egg noodles, boiled
1 tsp sesame oil, extra
$^{1}/_{2}$ red capsicum, seeded (extra) and chopped to garnish

1. Chop fish into bite-sized pieces. Heat enough vegetable oil to deep-fry fish for $2^{1}/_{2}$ minutes. Remove and drain. Cut green onions into 4cm sections, separating white parts from green.
2. Heat 3 tablespoons of oil and brown ginger and soften garlic. Add fish, bell pepper and white sections of green onions. Stir-fry for 3 minutes then add stock or water and boil. Add green scallion sections, oyster sauce, black pepper, oil and sherry and simmer for 1 minute, stirring.
3. Add hot, cooked, drained noodles and extra 1 teaspoon of oil. Stir through until hot. Serve immediately, garnished with chopped capsicum.

Serves 4

COOL CUMIN-SCENTED YOGHURT SOUP

Preparation 10 mins **Cooking** 7 mins + 1 hr blending **Calories** 355 **Fat** 9g

- 1 tsp cumin seeds
- 1 tsp nigella (black onion) seeds
- 1 tbsp ghee or butter
- 4 green onions, finely sliced
- 10 fresh mint leaves
- 2 tsps ground cumin
- 1 tsp turmeric
- 55g cashew nuts
- 285g canned chickpeas, drained and rinsed
- 2 cups plain low-fat yoghurt
- $^{4}/_{5}$ cup sour cream
- $^{4}/_{5}$ cup water
- 600g cucumbers
- 1 tbsp sugar
- salt and pepper, to taste
- 2 tbsps shredded coconut, toasted
- mint leaves, to garnish

1. Heat a stockpot (no oil) then add the cumin seeds and nigella seeds and toss them around the hot pan until they smell roasted and seem to 'pop' around the pan (about 3 minutes). Remove the seeds and set them aside.
2. Add the ghee or butter to the pot and add the finely sliced green onions and mint leaves and sauté for a few minutes until the green onions have wilted. Add the cumin, turmeric and cashew nuts and toss until the spices are fragrant and the nuts are golden. Add the drained chickpeas and cook for a further 2 minutes. Set aside.
3. In a mixing bowl, whisk together the yoghurt, sour cream and water until smooth. Season to taste with salt and pepper. Peel the cucumbers and scrape out the seeds. Cut the cucumber flesh into thin slices and add to the yoghurt mixture.
4. Add the onion/spice mixture to the yoghurt and stir thoroughly to combine all the delicious flavours. Allow the flavours to blend for 1 hour before serving. Garnish with toasted coconut, sliced mint leaves and a few nigella seeds.

Serves 4

Note: This traditional Muslim soup is served often during the month-long Ramadan when Muslims fast from sun up to sundown and therefore need a hearty evening meal.

THAI RICE SOUP WITH CHICKEN

Preparation 8 mins **Cooking** 30 mins **Calories** 190 **Fat** trace

$^{1}/_{2}$ cup raw rice
1 tbsp vegetable oil
1 large clove garlic, finely chopped
1 tbsp fresh ginger, finely grated
250g chicken thigh or breast fillets, trimmed and diced
white pepper, to taste
2 tbsps fish sauce
1 small onion, finely sliced
2 tbsps fresh coriander, chopped
2 tbsps green onions, chopped

Garnish
fresh coriander leaves
red chillies, finely sliced
green onions, sliced

1 Place rice in a large stockpot with 8 cups water and bring slowly to the boil. Simmer gently, adding more water as necessary so that mixture becomes a thin porridge consistency.

2 In a wok, large frying pan, or a stockpot heat the oil and stir-fry the garlic and ginger. Add the chicken and season with pepper and fish sauce. Add the onion and stir-fry until chicken is cooked, about 5 minutes. Stir into the rice stock. Just before serving, stir in the coriander and green onions. Ladle into heated bowls and garnish each with a few coriander leaves, chillies and green onions.

Serves 4

MIXED MUSHROOM NOODLE SOUP

Preparation 15 mins + standing **Cooking** 20 mins **Calories** 130 **Fat** trace

30g dried shiitake mushrooms
4 cups reduced salt vegetable stock
3cm piece ginger, crushed
1 halved garlic clove
1 whole star anise
1 tbsp reduced salt soy sauce
100g oyster mushrooms
400g fresh udon noodles
3 green onions, sliced
100g enoki mushrooms, gently separated

1. Put the shiitake mushrooms in an ovenproof bowl, add 1 cup boiling water and allow to stand for 25 minutes or until the mushrooms are soft. Drain, then strain and reserve the liquid. Cut the mushrooms into thin slices.
2. Put the stock, mushroom liquid, ginger, garlic, star anise and soy into a large pot and bring to the boil. Reduce the heat and simmer for 10 minutes. Remove the ginger, garlic and star anise and discard.
3. Add the oyster mushrooms, dried shiitake, udon noodles and green onions and simmer gently for 5 minutes.
4. Stir in the enoki and heat for 1 minute or until they soften. Serve hot.

Serves 6

CURRIED BROCCOLI AND SPLIT PEA SOUP WITH GARLIC NAAN

Preparation 15 mins **Cooking** 1 hr 15 mins **Calories** 416 **Fat** 8g

2 tsps corn oil
1 onion, sliced
1 tbsp Madras curry paste
1 cup yellow split peas
$^{1}/_{2}$ cup brown lentils
4 cups reduced salt vegetable stock
500g English spinach, washed and chopped
285g broccoli, cut into florets
1 tbsp lemon juice

Garlic Naan (Indian Bread)
2 plain naan or pita rounds
2 cloves garlic, crushed
1 tbsp corn oil
1 tsp cumin seeds

1. Heat the oil in a large stockpot, add the onion and curry paste and cook for a few minutes until the onion is soft and the curry paste is fragrant.
2. Add the split peas, lentils, vegetable stock and 2 cups water and bring to the boil, skimming occasionally to remove any scum. Cover and simmer for 1 hour or until both the peas and the lentils are quite soft.
3. Add the chopped spinach and broccoli and simmer for a couple of minutes until the broccoli is tender. Season with lemon juice.

Garlic Naan (Indian Bread)

1. To make the garlic naan: Preheat oven. Put the naan onto 2 non-stick baking trays, brush them with the combined garlic and oil, then sprinkle with cumin seeds. Wrap in foil and bake for 15 minutes or until warmed through. Cut into thick strips and serve hot with the soup.

Serves 6

Oven temperature 180°C, 350°F, Gas 4

THAI CHICKEN SOUP

Preparation 8 mins **Cooking** 10 mins **Calories** 211 **Fat** 3g

2 cups rediced salt chicken stock
2 kaffir lime or lemon myrtle leaves, optional
2 stalks fresh lemongrass or 2 tsps bottled lemongrass
1 bunch fresh coriander with roots
5 thin slices fresh galangal or ginger
1 skinless chicken breast fillet, cut into thin strips
2 shallots, sliced
2 fresh bird's eye chillies or pinch of sugar to taste
2 tbsps rice wine (mirin) or sherry
juice of 1 lime

1. Place stock and lime leaves in a large stockpot. Bring to the boil.
2. Meanwhile, remove the outer layers from the lemongrass. Chop. Cut the roots from two of the coriander plants. Chop. Remove leaves from remaining coriander. Set aside.
3. Place lemongrass, coriander roots and galangal or ginger in a mortar. Bruise with a pestle. Alternatively, place ingredients in a plastic food bag. Bruise with a rolling pin.
4. Stir lemongrass mixture into stock. Bring to simmering. Simmer for 2–3 minutes. Add chicken and shallots. Simmer for 5–6 minutes or until chicken is cooked.
5. Place reserved coriander leaves, chillies, sugar, fish sauce and lime juice in a small bowl. Mix to combine.
6. To serve, divide the mixture between warm soup bowls. Ladle over the soup. Mix gently to combine. For a main meal, serve with steamed jasmine rice.

Serves 2

GINGER CHICKEN WONTON SOUP

Preparation 10 mins **Cooking** 20 mins **Calories** 291 **Fat** 2g

Soup

1 tbsp sesame oil
1–2 tsps chilli paste
1 tbsp soy sauce
2 cloves garlic, minced
40g ginger, sliced
8 cups of chicken stock
200g can bamboo shoots
6 green onions, sliced diagonally

Wontons

4 fresh shiitake mushrooms
$^{1}/_{2}$ tsp Chinese five-spice powder
100g water chestnuts, drained
3 green onions, chopped
3 coriander, sprigs
2 tbsps soy sauce
1 tbsp fresh ginger, grated
1 fresh bird's eye chilli, minced
1 tbsp sesame seeds
2 chicken breast fillets, skin off
1 pack wonton wrappers

Soup

1. Heat the sesame oil in a stockpot and add the chilli paste, soy sauce and garlic and ginger and sauté for a moment or two. Add the stock and simmer for 15 minutes, then add the bamboo shoots and sliced green onions. Set aside.

Wontons

1. Place the all the ingredients except for the wonton wrappers in a food processor and 'pulse' the mixture until it is well chopped. Do not over-process.
2. To shape the wontons, separate wonton wrappers and lay them out on a bench. Place a $^{1}/_{2}$ tablespoon of filling in the centre of each wrapper. Working with one wrapper at a time, pick up the wrapper and moisten the edges with water. Fold the wrapper into a triangle, enclosing the filling and pinching the pastry together well to enclose the filling. Then wrap the triangle around your finger, carefully pinching together the opposite corners. Shape each wonton wrapper in this way.
3. Add the wontons to the simmering soup and cook them for about 4 minutes. Serve immediately.

Serves 6

Note: Home-made wonton soup is so simple to make, yet the complex flavours are so much more interesting than 'take-away' Chinese wonton soup. With wonton wrappers available from any Asian food store, you'll find this soup 'a snap' to prepare.

VELVET CHICKEN AND SWEET CORN SOUP

Preparation 15 mins **Cooking** 20 mins **Calories** 60 **Fat** 2g

500g boned chicken breast
large pinch of salt
2 egg whites, beaten to froth
6 cups chicken stock
400g can creamed corn
2 tbsp cornflour blended with $3^1/_2$ tbsps water
2 tbsp dry sherry
1 tbsp light soy sauce
1 tsp sesame oil
thin Chinese smoked ham or bacon, to garnish

1. Remove fat from chicken then mince, food process or finely chop until it is almost a purée. Mix in salt well and fold in egg whites. Bring stock to the boil, add corn and return soup to the boil.Thicken with cornflour mix, stirring for about 1 minute.
2. Stir in chicken purée, sherry, soy sauce and sesame oil and simmer, stirring, for 3 minutes. Serve soup (which is popular at formal banquets) garnished with finely chopped ham or cooked bacon bits. If you can't buy Chinese ham, substitute Virginia ham.

Serves 6

SPICY TOFU, MUSHROOM AND UDON SOUP

Preparation 10 mins marinating + 15 mins soaking **Cooking** 5 mins **Calories** 617 **Fat** 3g

200g firm tofu, diced
1 tbsp reduced salt soy sauce
1 tbsp sherry or rice wine
100g dried mushrooms, sliced or 4 whole dried mushrooms
1 lemon myrtle or kaffir lime leaf
2–3 tsps olive or peanut oil
2cm piece fresh ginger, thinly sliced
2 shallots, chopped or 1 spring onion, sliced diagonally
6 fresh shiitake or flat mushrooms, thinly sliced
2 cups shredded English spinach or bok choy
500g fresh udon noodles
4 cups hot chicken stock or dashi
1 tbsp cider vinegar

1. Place the tofu, soy sauce and sherry in a bowl. Toss to coat. Marinate for 10 minutes.
2. Place the dried mushrooms and lemon myrtle leaf in a separate bowl. Pour over 1/2 cup boiling water. Soak for 15 minutes or until mushrooms are tender.
3. Heat the oil in a wok or stockpot over a medium heat. Add the ginger, shallots and fresh mushrooms. Stir-fry for 1–2 minutes. Add spinach and tofu with marinade. Stir-fry for 1 minute.
4. Add noodles, dried mushrooms with their soaking water, stock and vinegar. Bring to the boil. Remove lemon myrtle leaf and discard. Serve immediately.

Serves 4

ORIENTAL NOODLE SOUP

Preparation 15 mins **Cooking** 30 mins **Calories** 150 **Fat** 2g

- 4 cups vegetable stock
- 125mL tamari
- 250g bean thread noodles
- 375g tofu, roughly chopped
- 155g bok choy, chopped
- 1 stalk fresh lemongrass, chopped, or 1 tsp dried lemongrass or 1 tsp lemon rind, finely grated
- 3 spring onions, sliced diagonally
- 5cm piece fresh ginger, sliced
- 200g straw or button mushrooms
- 1 tbsp fresh mint, chopped
- 2 tbsps fresh coriander, chopped
- 100g bean sprouts

1. Place stock and tamari in a large stockpot and bring to the boil. Reduce heat, add noodles, tofu, bok choy, lemongrass or lemon rind, spring onions, ginger, mushrooms, mint and coriander and simmer for 20 minutes.
2. To serve, divide bean sprouts between 4 warmed serving bowls and ladle over hot soup.

Serves 4

Note: Tamari is also called tamari shoyu or Japanese soy sauce. Made only from natural products, soya beans and salt, it contains no monosodium glutamate (MSG) which is often found in Chinese soy sauce. It is also lighter in flavour.

BALINESE EGG NOODLE SOUP

Preparation 12 mins **Cooking** 27 mins **Calories** 196 **Fat** 2.5g

2 carrots
1 sweet potato
145g Chinese cabbage
8 cups chicken or vegetable stock
8 spring onions (green parts only)
100g dried egg noodles
1 tbsp sweet soy sauce

Meatballs
6 shallots
4cm piece fresh ginger (3 tsps minced)
2 cloves garlic
2 tbsps olive oil
250g minced beef
2 tsps ground coriander
1 egg white
1 tbsp cornflour
salt and pepper, to taste

Garnish
2 onions, sliced and fried until crisp
1 red capsicum, finely shredded

Soup

1 Peel and finely chop the shallots, ginger and garlic. Heat the oil in the stockpot and sauté until these flavourings are softened. Remove 1/3 of this mixture and reserve for the meatballs.

2 To the remaining mixture, add the carrots and sweet potato (cut into matchsticks) and sauté for 5 minutes. Add the shredded cabbage and cook until wilted (about 4 minutes). Add the chicken/vegetable stock and the julienned greens and bring to the boil. Simmer for 10 minutes.

Meatballs

1 To the reserved shallot mixture, add the minced meat, coriander, egg white, cornflour, and salt and pepper to taste. Mix well and form into small balls.

2 To the simmering soup, add the meatballs and allow them to boil gently for a further 5 minutes. Add the noodles, pushing them down into the soup and simmer for a further 2 minutes or until the noodles are just tender.

3 Season with the sweet soy sauce and serve garnished with fried onions and julienne of capsicum.

Serves 6–8

THAI SPIKED PUMPKIN SOUP

Preparation 8 mins **Cooking** 2 hrs **Calories** 300 **Fat** 15g

- 2 tbsps olive oil
- 1 large brown onion
- 4 cloves garlic
- 1 small red bird's eye chilli
- 1/2 bunch coriander
- 1/2 tsp chilli paste
- 1 tsp ground cumin
- 1 tsp turmeric
- 500g pumpkin
- 500g butternut pumpkin
- 500g Japanese pumpkin
- 6 cups chicken stock
- 400g can coconut milk

1. Heat the olive oil in a large stockpot and add the onion and garlic and cook for 10 minutes to caramelise gently. Add the chilli and coriander stems (finely chopped) and stir until fragrant.
2. Add the remaining spices and heat until toasted. Add all the pumpkin pieces and stir to coat with the spice mixture. Cover with a lid and cook over a low heat for 30 minutes until the pumpkin is beginning to soften and turn brown. Add just enough stock to cover, and stir well.
3. Simmer for 1 hour, then add the coconut milk and simmer for a further 15 minutes. Purée then serve, garnished with extra chillies and coriander.

Serves 6

HOT AND SOUR CHICKEN SOUP

Preparation 10 mins **Cooking** 30 mins **Calories** 225 **Fat** 2g

600g chicken breast fillets (approx. 3)
2 tbsps peanut oil
4 cloves garlic, minced
2 shallots, chopped
5 stems of coriander, leaves included
30g piece ginger, bruised
3 small red Thai chillies, minced
3 stalks lemongrass, finely sliced
6 kaffir lime leaves, finely shredded*
8 cups chicken or vegetable stock
3 tbsps Thai fish sauce*
100g dry cellophane or glass noodles*
6 green onions, diagonally sliced
juice of 1–2 limes
handful of coriander leaves

1. Cut the chicken into 1cm thick strips. Brush the chicken strips with 1 tablespoon of peanut oil and grill or pan fry until the chicken is golden brown and slightly charred, about 3 minutes each side.
2. Heat the remaining tablespoon of peanut oil in a large stockpot and add the garlic, shallots, chopped coriander leaves and stems, ginger, minced chillies, sliced lemongrass and finely shredded lime leaves and toss in the hot oil until fragrant (about 2 minutes). Add the stock and bring to the boil. Simmer for 10 minutes then add the grilled chicken strips and simmer for a further 10 minutes.
3. Add the Thai fish sauce and noodles and simmer for a further two minutes, or until the noodles are tender.
4. Add the sliced spring onions, lime juice and coriander leaves and serve very hot.

Serves 6

*Available from Asian grocers/foodstores

GLOSSARY

Acidulated water: water with added acid, such as lemon juice or vinegar, which prevents discolouration of ingredients, particularly fruit or vegetables. The proportion of acid to water is 1 teaspoon per 300mL.

Al dente: Italian cooking term for ingredients that are cooked until tender but still firm to the bite; usually applied to pasta.

Américaine: method of serving seafood, usually lobster and monkfish, in a sauce flavoured with olive oil, aromatic herbs, tomatoes, white wine, fish stock, brandy and tarragon.

Anglaise: cooking style for simple cooked dishes such as boiled vegetables. Assiette anglaise is a plate of cold cooked meats.

Antipasto: Italian for 'before the meal', it denotes an assortment of cold meats, vegetables and cheeses, often marinated, served as an hors d'oeuvre. A typical antipasto might include salami, prosciutto, marinated artichoke hearts, anchovy fillets, olives, tuna fish and provolone cheese.

Au gratin: food sprinkled with breadcrumbs, often covered with cheese sauce and browned until a crisp coating forms.

Bain marie: a stockpot standing in a large pan which is filled with boiling water to keep liquids at simmering point. A double boiler will do the same job.

Balsamic vinegar: a mild, extremely fragrant, wine-based vinegar made in northern Italy. Traditionally, the vinegar is aged for at least seven years in a series of casks made of various woods.

Baste: to moisten food while it is cooking by spooning or brushing on liquid or fat.

Beat: to stir thoroughly and vigorously.

Beurre manie: equal quantities of butter and flour kneaded together and added, a little at a time, to thicken a stew or casserole.

bird: see paupiette.

Blanc: a cooking liquid made by adding flour and lemon juice to water in order to keep certain vegetables from discolouring as they cook.

Blanch: to plunge into boiling water and then, in some cases, into cold water. Fruits and nuts are blanched to remove skin easily.

Blanquette: a white stew of lamb, veal or chicken, bound with egg yolks and cream and accompanied by onion and mushrooms.

blend: to mix thoroughly.

Bonne femme: dishes cooked in the traditional French 'housewife' style. Chicken and pork bonne femme are garnished with bacon, potatoes and baby onion; fish bonne femme with mushrooms in a white-wine sauce.

Bouquet garni: a bunch of herbs, usually consisting of sprigs of parsley, thyme, marjoram, rosemary, a bay leaf, peppercorns and cloves, tied in muslin and used to flavour stews and casseroles.

Braise: to cook whole or large pieces of poultry, game, fish, meat or vegetables in a small amount of wine, stock or other liquid in a closed pot. Often the main ingredient is first browned in fat and then cooked in a low oven or very slowly on top of the stove. Braising suits tough meats and older birds and produces a mellow, rich sauce.

Broil: the American term for grilling food.

Brown: cook in a small amount of fat until brown.

Burghul (also bulgur): a type of cracked wheat, where the kernels are steamed and dried before being crushed.

Buttered: to spread with softened or melted butter.

Butterfly: to slit a piece of food in half horizontally, cutting it almost through so that when opened it resembles butterfly wings. Chops, large prawns and thick fish fillets are often butterflied so that they cook more quickly.

Buttermilk: a tangy, low-fat cultured milk product; its slight acidity makes it an ideal marinade base for poultry.

Calzone: a semicircular pocket of pizza dough, stuffed with meat or vegetables, sealed and baked.

Caramelise: to melt sugar until it is a golden-brown syrup.

Champignons: small mushrooms, usually canned.

Chasseur: French for 'hunter'; a French cooking style in which meat and chicken dishes are cooked with mushrooms, spring onions, white wine and often tomato.

Clarify: to melt butter and drain the oil off the sediment.

Coat: to cover with a thin layer of flour, sugar, nuts, crumbs, poppy or sesame seeds, cinnamon sugar or a few of the ground spices.

Concasser: to chop coarsely, usually tomatoes.

Confit: from the French verb confire, meaning to preserve, food that is made into a preserve by cooking very slowly and thoroughly until tender. In the case of meat, such as duck or goose, it is cooked in its own fat, and covered with the fat so that the meat does not come into contact with the air. Vegetables such as onions are good in confit.

Consommé: a clear soup usually made from beef.

Coulis: a thin purée, usually of fresh or cooked fruit or vegetables, which is soft enough to pour (in French couler means 'to run'). A coulis may be rough-textured or very smooth.

Court bouillon: the liquid in which fish, poultry or meat is cooked. It usually consists of water with bay leaf, onion, carrots and salt and freshly ground black pepper to taste. Other additives may include wine, vinegar, stock, garlic or spring (green) onions.

Couscous: cereal processed from semolina into pellets, traditionally steamed and served with meat and vegetables in the classic North African stew of the same name.

Cream: to make soft, smooth and creamy by rubbing with the back of a spoon or by beating with a mixer. Usually applied to fat and sugar.

Croutons: small toasted or fried cubes of bread.

Cruciferous vegetables: certain members of the mustard, cabbage and turnip families with cross-shaped flowers and strong aromas and flavours.

Crudités: raw vegetables, cut in slices or sticks to nibble plain or with a dipping sauce, or shredded vegetables tossed as salad with a simple dressing.

Cube: to cut into small pieces with six equal sides.

Curdle: to cause milk or sauce to separate into solid and liquid. Example, overcooked egg mixtures.

Daikon radish (also called mooli): a long white Japanese radish.

Dark sesame oil (also called Oriental sesame oil): dark polyunsaturated oil with a low burning point, used for seasoning. Do not replace with lighter sesame oil.

Deglaze: to dissolve congealed cooking juices or glaze on the bottom of a pan by adding a liquid, then scraping and stirring vigorously whilst bringing the liquid to the boil. Juices may be used to make gravy or to add to sauce.

Degrease: to skim grease from the surface of liquid. If possible the liquid should be chilled so the fat solidifies. If not, skim off most of the fat with a large metal spoon, then trail strips of paper towel on the surface of the liquid to remove any remaining globules.

Devilled: a dish or sauce that is highly seasoned with a hot ingredient such as mustard, Worcestershire sauce or cayenne pepper.

Dice: to cut into small cubes.

Dietary fibre: a plant-cell material that is undigested or only partially digested in the human body, but which promotes healthy digestion of other food matter.

Dissolve: mix a dry ingredient with liquid until absorbed.

Dredge: to coat with a dry ingredient, such as flour or sugar.

Drizzle: to pour in a fine thread-like stream over a surface.

Dust: to sprinkle or coat lightly with flour or icing sugar.

Dutch oven: a heavy casserole with a lid usually made from cast iron or pottery.

Emulsion: a mixture of two liquids that are not mutually soluble; for example, oil and water.

Entrée: in Europe, the 'entry' or hors d'oeuvre; in North America entree means the main course.

Fenugreek: a small, slender annual herb of the pea family. The seeds are spice. Ground fenugreek has a strong maple sweetness, spicy but bitter flavour and an aroma of burnt sugar.

Fillet: special cut of beef, lamb, pork or veal; breast of poultry and game; fish cut off the bone lengthwise.

Flake: to break into small pieces with a fork.

Flame: to ignite warmed alcohol over food.

Fold in: a gentle, careful combining of a light or delicate mixture with a heavier mixture, using a metal spoon.

Frenched: when fat and gristle is scraped and cut from meat on a bone, leaving the meaty part virtually fat free.

Fricassé: a dish in which poultry, fish or vegetables are bound together with a white or velouté sauce. In Britain and the United States, the name applies to an old-fashioned dish of chicken in a creamy sauce.

Galangal: A member of the ginger family, commonly known as Laos or Siamese ginger. It has a peppery taste with overtones of ginger.

Galette: sweet or savoury mixture shaped as a flat round.

Ganache: a filling or glaze made of full cream, chocolate, and/or other flavourings, often used to sandwich the layers of gourmet chocolate cakes

Garnish: to decorate food, usually with something edible.

Gastrique: caramelised sugar deglazed with vinegar and used in fruit-flavoured savoury sauces, in such dishes as duck with orange.

Ghee: butter, clarified by boiling. Commonly used in Indian cooking.

Glaze: a thin coating of beaten egg, syrup or aspic which is brushed over pastry, fruits or cooked meats.

Gluten: a protein in flour that is developed when dough is kneaded, making the dough elastic.

Gratin: a dish cooked in the oven or under the grill so that it develops a brown crust. Breadcrumbs or cheese may be sprinkled on top first. Shallow gratin dishes ensure a maximum area of crust.

Grease: to rub or brush lightly with oil or fat.

Infuse: to immerse herbs, spices or other flavourings in hot liquid to flavour it. Infusion takes 2–5 minutes depending on the flavouring. The liquid should be very hot but not boiling.

Jardinière: a garnish of garden vegetables, typically carrots, pickling onions, French beans and turnips.

Joint: to cut poultry, game or small animals into serving pieces by dividing at the joint.

Julienne: to cut food into match-like strips.

Lights: lungs of an animal, used in various meat preparations such as pates and faggots.

Line: to cover the inside of a container with paper, to protect or aid in removing mixture.

Knead: to work dough using heel of hand with a pressing motion, while stretching and folding the dough.

Macerate: to soak food in liquid to soften.

Marinade: a seasoned liquid, usually an oil and acid mixture, in which meats or other foods are soaked to soften and give more flavour.

Marinara: Italian 'sailor's style' cooking that does not apply to any particular combination of ingredients. Marinara tomato sauce for pasta is the most familiar.

Marinate: to let food stand in a marinade to season and tenderise.

Mask: to cover cooked food with sauce.

Melt: to heat until liquified.

Mince: to grind into very small pieces.

Mix: to combine ingredients by stirring.

Monounsaturated fats: one of three types of fats found in foods. It is believed these fats do not raise the level of cholesterol in the blood.

Naan: a slightly leavened bread used in Indian cooking.

Niçoise: a garnish of tomatoes, garlic and black olives; a salad with anchovy, tuna and French beans is typical.

Noisette: small 'nut' of lamb cut from boned loin or rack that is rolled, tied and cut in neat slices. Noisette also means flavoured with hazelnuts, or butter cooked to a nut brown colour.

Non-reactive pan: a cooking pan whose surface does not chemically react with food. Materials used include stainless steel, enamel, glass and some alloys.

Normande: a cooking style for fish, with a garnish of prawn, mussels and mushrooms in a white-wine cream sauce; for poultry and meat, a sauce with cream, calvados and apple.

Olive oil: various grades of oil extracted from olives. Extra virgin olive oil has a full, fruity flavour and the lowest acidity. Virgin olive oil is slightly higher in acidity and lighter in flavour. Pure olive oil is a processed blend of olive oils and has the highest acidity and lightest taste.

Panade: a mixture for binding stuffings and dumplings, notably quenelles (fish rissoles), often of choux pastry or simply breadcrumbs. A panade may also be made of frangipane, puréed potatoes or rice.

Papillote: to cook food in oiled or buttered greasepoof paper or aluminum foil. Also a decorative frill to cover bone ends of chops and poultry drumsticks.

Parboil: to boil or simmer until part cooked (i.e. cooked further than when blanching).

Pare: to cut away outside covering.

Pâté: a paste of meat or seafood used as a spread for toast or crackers.

Paupiette: a thin slice of meat, poultry or fish spread with a savoury stuffing and rolled. In the United States this is also called 'bird' and in Britain an 'olive'.

Peel: to strip away outside covering.

Plump: to soak in liquid or moisten thoroughly until full and round.

Poach: to simmer gently in enough hot liquid to cover, using care to retain shape of food.

Polyunsaturated fat: one of the three types of fats found in food. These exist in large quantities in such vegetable oils as safflower, sunflower, corn and soya bean. These fats lower the level of cholesterol in the blood.

Purée: a smooth paste, usually of vegetables or fruits, made by putting foods through a sieve, food mill or liquefying in a blender or food processor.

Ragout: traditionally a well-seasoned, rich stew containing meat, vegetables and wine. Nowadays, a term applied to any stewed mixture.

Ramekins: small oval or round individual baking dishes.

Reconstitute: to put moisture back into dehydrated foods by soaking in liquid.

Reduce: to cook over a very high heat, uncovered, until the liquid is reduced by evaporation.

Refresh: to cool hot food quickly, either under running water or by plunging it into iced water, to stop it cooking. Particularly for vegetables and occasionally for shellfish.

Rice vinegar: mild, fragrant vinegar that is less sweet than cider vinegar and not as harsh as distilled malt vinegar. Japanese rice vinegar is milder than the Chinese variety.

Roulade: a piece of meat, usually pork or veal, that is spread with stuffing, rolled and often braised or poached. A roulade may also be a sweet or savoury mixture that is baked in a Swiss-roll tin or paper case, filled with a contrasting filling, and rolled.

Roux: A binding for sauces, made with flour and butter or another fatty substance, to which a hot liquid is added. A roux-based sauce may be white, blond or brown, depending on how the butter has been cooked.

Rubbing-in: a method of incorporating fat into flour, by use of fingertips only. Also incorporates air into mixture.

Safflower oil: the vegetable oil that contains the highest proportion of polyunsaturated fats.

Salsa: a juice derived from the main ingredient being cooked, or a sauce added to a dish to enhance its flavour. In Italy the term is often used for pasta sauces; in Mexico the name usually applies to uncooked sauces served as an accompaniment, especially to corn chips.

Saturated fats: one of the three types of fats found in foods. These exist in large quantities in animal products, coconut and palm oils; they raise the level of cholesterol in the blood. As high cholesterol levels may cause heart disease, saturated-fat consumption is recommended to be less than 15 percent of calories provided by the daily diet.

Sauté: to cook or brown in small amount of hot fat.

Scald: to bring just to boiling point, usually for milk. Also to rinse with boiling water.

School prawns: delicious eaten just on their own. Smaller prawn than bay, tiger or king. They have a mild flavour, low oiliness and high moisture content, they make excellent cocktails.

Score: to mark food with cuts, notches or lines to prevent curling or to make food more attractive.

Sear: to brown surface quickly over high heat in hot dish.

Seasoned flour: flour with salt and pepper added.

Sift: to shake a dry, powdered substance through a sieve or sifter to remove any lumps and give lightness.

Simmer: to cook food gently in liquid that bubbles steadily just below boiling point so that the food cooks in even heat without breaking up.

Singe: to quickly flame poultry to remove all traces of feathers after plucking.

Skim: to remove a surface layer (often of impurities and scum) from a liquid with a metal spoon or small ladle.

Slivered: sliced in long, thin pieces, usually refers to nuts, especially almonds.

Souse: to cover food, particularly fish, in wine vinegar and spices and cook slowly; the food is cooled in the same liquid. Sousing gives food a pickled flavour.

Steep: to soak in warm or cold liquid in order to soften food and draw out strong flavours or impurities.

Stir-fry: to cook thin slices of meat and vegetable over a high heat in a small amount of oil, stirring constantly to even cooking in a short time. Traditionally cooked in a wok; however, a heavy-based frying pan may be used.

Stock: the liquid that results from cooking meat, bones and/or vegetables in water to make a base for soups and other recipes. You can substitute stock cubes for fresh bouillon, but those on a reduced sodium diet will need to take note of the salt content on the packet.

Stud: to adorn with; for example, baked ham studded with whole cloves.

Sugo: an Italian sauce made from the liquid or juice extracted from fruit or meat during cooking.

Sweat: to cook sliced or chopped food, usually vegetables, in a little fat and no liquid over very low heat. Foil is pressed on top so that the food steams in its own juices, usually before being added to other dishes.

Thicken: to make a liquid thicker by mixing together arrowroot, cornflour or flour with an equal amount of cold water and pouring it into hot liquid, cooking and stirring until thickened.

Timbale: a creamy mixture of vegetables or meat baked in a mould. French for 'kettledrum'; also denotes a drum-shaped baking dish.

Toss: to gently mix ingredients with two forks or fork and spoon.

Total fat: the individual daily intake of all three fats previously described in this glossary. Nutritionists recommend that fats provide no more than 35 percent of the energy in the diet.

Vine leaves: tender, lightly flavoured leaves of the grapevine, used in ethnic cuisine as wrappers for savoury mixtures. As the leaves are usually packed in brine, they should be well rinsed before use.

Whip: to beat rapidly, incorporate air and produce expansion.

Zest: thin outer layer of citrus fruits containing the aromatic citrus oil. It is usually thinly pared with a vegetable peeler, or grated with a zester or grater to separate it from the bitter white pith underneath.

WEIGHTS AND MEASURES

Cooking is not an exact science; one does not require finely calibrated scales, pipettes and scientific equipment to cook, yet the conversion to metric measures in some countries and its interpretations must have intimidated many a good cook.

In the recipes weights are given for ingredients such, as meats, fish, poultry and some vegetables, but in normal cooking a few ounces or grams one way or another will not affect the success of your dish.

Although recipes have been tested using the Australian Standard 250mL cup, 20mL tablespoon and 5mL teaspoon, they will work just as well with the US and Canadian 8fl oz cup, or the UK 300mL cup. We have used graduated cup measures in preference to tablespoon measures so that proportions are always the same. Where tablespoon measures have been given, they are not crucial measures, so using the smaller tablespoon of the US or UK will not affect the recipe's success. At least we all agree on the teaspoon size.

For breads, cakes and pastries, the only area which might cause concern is where eggs are used, as proportions will then vary. If working with a 250mL or 300mL cup, use large eggs (65g/2$^1/_4$oz), adding a little more liquid to the recipe for 300mL cup measures if it seems necessary. Use the medium-sized eggs (55g/2oz) with 8fl oz cup measure. A graduated set of measuring cups and spoons is recommended, the cups in particular for measuring dry ingredients. Remember to level such ingredients to ensure an accurate quantity.

English Measures

All measurements are similar to Australian with two exceptions: the English cup measures 300mL/10$^1/_2$ fl oz, whereas the American and Australian cup measure 250mL/8$^3/_4$fl oz. The English tablespoon (the Australian dessertspoon) measures 14.8mL /$^1/_2$ fl oz against Australian tablespoon of 20mL/$^3/_4$fl oz. The Imperial measurement is 20fl oz to the pint, 40fl oz a quart and 160fl oz one gallon.

American Measures

The American reputed pint is 16fl oz, a quart is equal to 32fl oz and the American gallon, 128fl oz. The American tablespoon is equal to 14.8mL/$^1/_2$ fl oz, the teaspoon is 5mL/$^1/_6$ fl oz. The cup measure is 250 mL/8$^3/_4$ fl oz.

Dry Measures

All the measures are level, so when you have filled a cup or spoon, level it off with the edge of a knife. The scale below is the 'cook's equivalent'; it is not an exact conversion of metric to imperial measurement. To calculate the exact metric equivalent yourself, multiply onces x 28.349523 to obtain grams, or divide 28.349523 grams to obtain onces.

Metric grams (g), kilograms (kg)	Imperial ounces (oz), pound (lb)
15g	$^1/_2$oz
20g	$^1/_3$oz
30g	1oz
55g	2oz
85g	3oz
115g	4oz/$^1/_4$ lb
125g	4$^1/_2$oz
140/145g	5oz
170g	6oz
200g	7oz
225g	8oz/$^1/_2$ lb
315g	11oz
340g	12oz/$^3/_4$ lb
370g	13oz
400g	14oz
425g	15oz
455g	16oz/1 lb
1,000g/1kg	35.3oz/2.2 lb
1.5kg	3.33 lb

Oven Temperatures

The Celsius temperatures given here are not exact; they have been rounded off and are given as a guide only. Follow the manufacturer's temperature guide, relating it to oven description given in the recipe. Remember gas ovens are hottest at the top, electric ovens at the bottom and convection-fan forced ovens are usually even throughout. We included Regulo numbers for gas cookers which may assist. To convert °C to °F multiply °C by 9 and divide by 5 then add 32.

	C°	F°	Gas regulo
Very slow	120	250	1
Slow	150	300	2
Moderately slow	160	325	3
Moderate	180	350	4
Moderately hot	190–200	370–400	5–6
Hot	210–220	410–440	6–7
Very hot	230	450	8
Super hot	250–290	475–500	9–10

Cup Measurements

One cup is equal to the following weights.

	Metric	Imperial
Almonds, flaked	85g	3oz
Almonds, slivered, ground	125g	4 1/2oz
Almonds, kernel	155g	5 1/2oz
Apples, dried, chopped	125g	4 1/2oz
Apricots, dried, chopped	190g	6 3/4oz
Breadcrumbs, packet	125g	4 1/2oz
Breadcrumbs, soft	55g	2oz
Cheese, grated	115g	4oz
Choc bits	155 1/2g	5oz
Coconut, desiccated	90g	3oz
Cornflakes	30g	1oz
Currants	155 1/2g	5oz
Flour	115g	4oz
Fruit, dried (mixed, sultanas etc)	170g	6 oz
Ginger, crystallised, glace	250g	8oz
Honey, treacle, golden syrup	315g	11oz
Mixed peel	225g	8oz
Nuts, chopped	115g	4oz
Prunes, chopped	225g	8oz
Rice, cooked	155g	5 1/2oz
Rice, uncooked	225g	8oz
Rolled oats	90g	3oz
Sesame seeds	115g	4oz
Shortening (butter, margarine)	225g	8oz
Sugar, brown	155g	5 1/2oz
Sugar, granulated or caster	225g	8oz
Sugar, sifted icing	155g	5 1/2oz
Wheatgerm	60g	2oz

Length

Some of us still have trouble converting imperial length to metric. In this scale, measures have been rounded off to the easiest-to-use and most acceptable figures. To obtain the exact metric equivalent in converting inches to centimetres, multiply inches by 2.54 whereby 1 inch equals 25.4 millimetres and 1 millimetre equals 0.03937 inches.

Cake Dish Sizes

Metric	15cm	18cm	20cm	20cm
Imperial	6in	7in	8in	9in

Loaf Dish Sizes

Metric	23 x 12cm	25 x 8cm	28 x18cm
Imperial	9 x 5in	10 x 3in	11 x 7in

Liquid Measures

Metric millilitres (mL)	Imperial fluid ounce (fl oz)	Cup and Spoon
5mL	1/6 fl oz	1 teaspoon
20mL	2/3 fl oz	1 tablespoon
30mL	1 fl oz	1 tbsp + 2tsp
55mL	2 fl oz	
63mL	2 1/4 fl oz	1/4 cup
85mL	3 fl oz	
115mL	4 fl oz	
125mL	4 1/2 fl oz	1/2 cup
150mL	5 1/4 fl oz	
188mL	6 2/3 fl oz	3/4 cup
225mL	8 fl oz	
250mL	8 3/4 fl oz	1 cup
300mL	10 1/2 fl oz	
370mL	13 fl oz	
400mL	14 fl oz	
438mL	15 1/2 fl oz	1 3/4 cups
455mL	16 fl oz	
500mL	17 1/2 fl oz	2 cups
570mL	0 fl oz	
1 litre	35.3 fl oz	4 cups

Length Measures

Metric millimetres (mm), centimetres (cm)	Imperial inches (in), feet (ft)
5mm, 0.5cm	1/4 in
10mm, 1.0cm	1/2 in
20mm, 2.0cm	3/4 in
2.5cm	1in
5 cm	2in
7 1/2 cm	3in
10cm	4in
12 1/2 cm	5in
15cm	6in
18cm	7in
20cm	8in
23cm	9in
25cm	10in
28cm	11in
30cm	12in, 1 foot

INDEX